The Pythagorean Silence

A Treatise on the Soul

by

Ross Lee Graham, Ph.D.

...I do not think it a good thing for men that there should be a disquisition, as it is called, on this topic--except for some few, who are able with a little teaching to find it out for themselves.
-- Plato, *The Seventh Letter*.

Time-Module Books
Braşov, Transylvania

The Pythagorean Silence
A Treatise on the Soul

All Rights Reserved © 2007 by Ross Lee Graham, PhD

Time-Module Books
Published in Braşov, Transylvania

Printed in the USA by lulu.com

DISCLAIMER: The readers who pursue the Pythagorean Silence through the use of this book do so *at their own risk*. The goal of the Pythagorean Silence is to recollect the Communion of the individual soul and the Universal Soul. Readers of this book are NOT and cannot be offered any guarantee of success in this endeavor; and the phrase *at their own risk* implies and dictates that the readers waive any claim for damages that might ensue through their use of this book.

ISBN 978-0-6152-1814-4

Distributed by Barnes & Noble

Pythagorean Silence
A Treatise on the Soul

TABLE OF CONTENTS

...everything that comes into being comes into being from its contrary...

— Aristotle, *On the Heavens*

Prologue

The Pythagorean sign is the Pentacle. In part, this sign is chosen because of the many ways its sections can express the ratio of the Golden Mean.

Pythagoras invented two words to distinguish two sections for his school, the *exoteric* and the *esoteric*. The exoteric section was more visible to the world and it was regarded as the groundwork school. It was a five year program that included thought control disciplines that prepared the way for the Pythagorean Silence. The esoteric section consisted of students initiated into the more secretive learning and practices after completing the exoteric preparations. The secrecy was a protection against outside prejudice and abuse of this learning.

> **Note:** The exoteric school preparatory program also includes subjects that are outside the scope of this treatise. These other subjects are found in the Trivium and the Quadrivium. The Trivium includes Logic, Grammar, and Rhetoric. The Quadrivium includes the study of Geometry, Astronomy, Arithmetic, and Music. Astronomy is regarded as Geometry in motion. Music is regarded as Arithmetic in motion.

The first four Lessons herein relate thought control disciplines that are consistent with Pythagorean exoteric practices. The underpinning logic of these preparatory exercises is well known to schools that practice the Pythagorean doctrine. One of the unhidden schools was founded in Europe by Gurdieff. His disciple, Ouspenski, penned the public aspects of this school in a number of his books. One entitled, *The Fourth Way*, included the Law of Three and the Law of Seven imbedded in some of the Pythagorean themes of cosmology and music.

A number of Ouspenski's books relate much on the exoteric aspect of mechanical existence. He describes the means for unifying the self and the practice of self-remembering that can put us in control of our mechanical existence. Though this aspect of training is important to the Pythagorean school, it remains the exoteric aspect and does not explicitly lead toward the Pythagorean Silence and therefore does not explicitly lead toward liberation from mechanical existence. Neither Gurdieff nor Ouspenski speak of the Communion of the individual soul with the Universal Soul.

The Gurdieff esoteric school teaching remains obfuscated in his *All and Everything* and his Beelzebub stories. There is no indication that he ever tutored anyone in how to interpret these stories. Thus by all public notice the school seems to have no completion. This was the major complaint of Ouspenski who broke away from the original school to teach what he knew. Ouspenski died believing that his knowledge of the Gurdieff school was incomplete. Descendents of the original Gurdieff school still have meetings in Paris, France (not to be confused with a New York group founded by Ouspenski that moved to the Paris region).

Plato and Pythagoras. 'Plato' (meaning 'broad shouldered') was the nickname of a man named Aristes. All of his family that we know about respected Pythagoreans. Many of the influential people of Athens in Plato's time were Pythagorean. Socrates is reported by Plato to have said. "The unexamined life is not worth living." This is a foundational precept of the Pythagoreans.

Of all the known dialogues of Plato, Pythagoras is only mentioned by name in 'The Republic'. The cave allegory in that work (Book VII) derives from Pythagorean beliefs. At the time of Plato, the Pythagoreans had a well established system of practicing the Pythagorean Silence. They established deep caves where they could retreat for minimal input, a kind of sensory deprivation environment.

> **Note:** Anyone who attempts a sensory deprivation experience without thought control training may only obtain dangerous levels of disorientation. It usually takes several years of training in thought control for the silence to be completed correctly.

'Pythagorean Silence' did not mean stop talking. It meant to quiet all input. The body is our sensory organ for the world around us and in its sensory function it can distract us from recollecting the Communion of the individual soul and the Universal Soul. The practice of this silence is to eliminate any obstruction to this recollection.

Furthermore, it should be clear that the exercise of silence is not the goal. It is taught that with sufficient practice one can maintain the recollection of Communion in daily life. Therefore, any retreat designed to facilitate this recollection is a temporary retreat. Re-entry into daily life is always expected, though with a difference.

If you read Plato's cave 'allegory' (*Republic*, Book VII) with this in mind you may find it easier to see it as a Pythagorean allegory. Plato's *Republic* is followed by *Timaeus*, named after one of Plato's Pythagorean relations, who outlines the Pythagorean design of the Universe.

> **Note:** Some scholars claim that Timaeus is a fiction invented by Plato. This is inconsistent with all of his other dialogues that are now titled with names of people. Timaeus would be the only one that is fictional.

The Historical Arguments section (below) points with some force toward the conclusion that the *Yoga Sutras* of Patanjali originated with the Pythagorean school. The text that represents the complete outline of the Pythagorean esoteric teaching is herein presented in Lesson 5. No commentaries contemporary with these Sutras exist.

The Pythagoreans, as is the custom in their schools, do not present the text with written commentaries. This is to encourage dialogue and avoid turning the understanding into a mechanistic learning process. The students memorize the 'Sutras' (mechanical aspect) and each Sutra is examined in dialogue (non-mechanical aspect), often with a tutor who keeps the dialogue on the subject at hand and keeps the dialogue going with questions. The emphasis in this method is self-discovery, a mode of learning that the Pythagoreans characterize as *Recollection*. The Sutras then become mnemonic devices to recall these discoveries, and this includes an understanding on how to achieve the Pythagorean Silence.

One of the mechanical methods for emphasis in teaching any doctrine is repetition. A scholarly presentation would avoid such repetitions. All of the main themes of the Pythagorean Doctrine are repeated throughout this text. The intent is to render the text useful more as a practical guide than a scholarly guide. These repetitions often appear in variations of context that suggest different ways of viewing the themes. I offer no apology for any of these repetitions.

All readers should read the Disclaimer on the copyright page before proceeding to the main text.

Ross Lee Graham, PhD
drrosslg@yahoo.com
West Bengal, India

Historical Arguments

From Pythagoras to Patanjali

Abstract. *While studying Sanskrit and 10th Century Tibetan in India, I studied the Patanjali Yoga Sutras. I saw in them affinities to ideas I associated with Pythagoras. I suspected a relation that is closer than mere coincidence. Some Sanskrit textbooks mention certain changes in consonants such as the /r/ changing to /l/. Based on this and some further geographic consonant transitions in place-names from West to East of the Indus river I applied these changes to the name of 'Pythagoras' and compared the result with 'Patanjali'. There appeared for me an argument in favor of interpreting 'Patanjali' as a phonetic transition from 'Pythagoras'. This, with some arguments based on text content and certain historical events, supplied sufficient evidence for serious consideration.*

> **Note:** There is also a Sanskrit grammarian with the name Patanjali. The following arguments deny that he is the same person as the Patanjali of the *Yoga Sutras*. Giving famous names to children is common practice in many cultures.

Introduction. An ambition of Aristotle was to unite the learning of the entire world. His student, Alexander the Great was inspired by this idea and ancillary to his world conquests proceeded to carry it out. Alexander started his conquest of the known world in 334 B.C. A few years later (331 B.C.) he founded the city of Alexandria in Egypt. With this city named after himself, he founded the first great library for uniting the learning of the known world. Other cities were founded by him, all together seventeen were named Alexandria, and he also founded more libraries. They functioned as book depositories, translation centers, and became known centers of learning. The two best known were the one in Alexandria, Egypt, and the one in Alexandria, Bactria (now Kandahar, Afghanistan).

One of the great sources of Greek influence on Eastern culture is Bactria (conquered by Alexander in 329 B.C.), situated north of the Hindu Kush Mountains. This is where Alexander married Roxanne (a Sogdian). The territory is now divided into Afghanistan, Uzbekistan, and Turkmenistan. Its capitol, Bactra (now Balkh, Afghanistan) may have cradled the Zarathustran religion. The Seleucid Empire took over this area after Alexander's death. This dynasty was founded by one of Alexander's Macedonian generals, Seleucis I, who inherited the ambition to unite the cultures and learning of the world. He strongly supported the libraries.

Bactria became independent under Diodotus I, 238 B.C. This independence was maintained until it was overrun by Sakas, 130 B.C.

Sanskrit. There is clear evidence that Sanskrit was not a natural language of old India. Current belief is that it came into India proper (the territory that today we know as India) with the alleged Aryan invasions. However, there is no evidence of any Aryan invasion prior to 326 B.C.

Panini increased the difficulty of establishing definitive ancient texts when he 'normalized' the Sanskrit language into about 4000 rules. This was followed by a concerted effort of many Indian scholars to 'normalize' all Sanskrit texts in accordance with the Panini Sanskrit Sutras. Very few texts are left unscathed by this artificial purification of Sanskrit. In large part, tradition has it that the Rigvedas escaped this Paninization because the Brahmin wanted to conserve their holy scriptures in their earliest Sanskrit rendition (we do not know what the original language is for the Rigvedas). Panini conformed somewhat to this demand by including rules that only refer to Rigveda structures, a necessity for Brahmin acceptance.

> **Note:** This assumes the conservation of Brahmin scriptures in a Sanskrit rendering. If Sanskrit was not available before contact with Aryan people then either the Rigvidas are non-Indian or their original language was not Sanskrit.

Ancient Persian and unscathed Sanskrit are not very different. We do not know when the Rigvedas were rendered into Sanskrit. It is not a necessary conclusion that all early Sanskrit texts derive from the ancient Persian culture. We also know that an Alexandrian library function was to translate Greek texts into Persian and Persian texts into Greek. The violence of history has made it difficult to measure the extent of this achievement.

It is not far-fetched to assume that much of the Greek influence on Indian religion, philosophy and literature comes through the Alexandrian translations. Much of this is documented but there is more work to be done. The Hindu caste system may actually come through a Greek source. In Plato's *Timaeus* (§24), Critias speaks of four castes: priests, warriors, artificers, shepherds-hunters-husbandmen. The Indian castes correspond rather well to these recorded by Plato. There are Indian gods that seem to be modified forms of Greek gods or Greek mythic characters. It is known that at the time of Alexander the Great the caste system was not yet well defined in Indian culture (more details in Epilogue). These and other studies are open ground for further work.

It is more than likely that Pythagorean texts were available to Alexander the Great. If this is the case then it is probable that the available Pythagorean texts were stored, copied, and translated in his libraries. Therefore, these Pythagorean texts would be available in local language translations. This is consistent with the original intent behind Alexander's library system.

The Pythagorean exoteric school though selective was more public and open to many who hoped to prepare for the esoteric school. The esoteric school was for a chosen few and secretive. We do not know the details of policy for the secret documents in Alexander's libraries. Secrecy has a function that is counter to the goal to unite the learning of the entire world. Even if the libraries began by respecting Pythagorean secrets, time and events may have withered the secrecy.

These Alexandrian libraries were still functioning under the Seleucid Empire when the *Yoga Sutras* of Patanjali became known to Indian commentators circa 200 B.C.

These great libraries of Alexander the Great have all been destroyed. Their demise represents a tragic loss to world history. We only have echoes of what these great learning centers had been.

Pythagoras. Pythagoras is known as a Greek philosopher and mathematician, born in Samos. Sources indicate that he was influenced by the early Ionian philosophers Thales, Anaximander, and Anaximenes. We have hearsay evidence that in revulsion for the tyranny of Polycrates (c522 B.C.) he left Samos. He settled in Crotona, a Greek colony in Italy. There he founded a school that promulgated what we have come to know as Pythagorean.

It is reported that Pythagoras claimed to remember all of his previous existences and thought that in an identity from a previous life he was Euphorbus, a warrior in the Trojan War.

The date for Pythagoras is difficult to pinpoint, though we are sure of the epoch. The present estimate is c582—500 B.C. Most scholars accept that there is adequate historical evidence for his existence.

Patanjali. There is great difficulty in trying to correlate Patanjali with Indian literature of any certain epoch. For Dasgupta (respected Indian historian) there is sufficient evidence to suggest that Patanjali did not write his *Yoga Sutras* later than about 200 B.C. Though this helps establish a guess for when the work began to influence Indian authors, it provides no reliable proof that the work originated in India. It helps the claim that the work comes forward and appears in ancient times when the Alexandrian libraries were still in full operation, but the date remains inconclusive. Furthermore, from Dasgupta's lengthy discussion of sparse evidence we cannot deny the possibility that these *Sutras* were not of Indian origin.

Following the arguments of Dasgupta it becomes apparent that Patanjali does not have a well-defined position in the historical context of India. There is not even one scrap of evidence concerning where he was born, how he lived, or where he died. The date for his work remains vague. Though dating early Indian works is often problematic, for this case it seems that the difficulties are generated because Patanjali was not Indian. In this regard there is further circumstantial evidence that leans toward this conclusion.

Linguistic Geographic Transition: Crossing the Indus river from West to East the name 'Pythagoras' could have changed to 'Patanjali'. One of the case studies for geographic transitions of consonants in place-names in Phonetics considers the changes in consonants of ancient languages from West to East across the Indus. This proposed phonetic transition only includes a few consonants in place-name words, i.e., the vowels are ignored. The best documented changes are, the /r/ changes to /l/, and the final /s/ is dropped. For the other consonants, in Sanskrit the theta sound does not exist and therefore a /th/ likely changes to a /t/. The /g/ to /nj/ is more speculative and may relate phonemically to /ng/ that derives from the Greek digamma form. These changes transliterate 'Pythagoras' into 'Pytangola' or 'Pytanjola'. Following this logic in the reverse direction suggests that 'Patanjali' comes from 'Patagaris' (or 'Pathagaris'), etc. Together these suggest a correspondence, and when taken with other circumstantial evidence it seems likely too close for coincidence.

> **NOTE:** It may be asked by the novice how is it that an Author's name can change through this geographic spread while the text itself may not exhibit such changes. As was the custom at the time, the Author's name was never written on the manuscript. It was up to the student to memorize the genealogy of teachers up to the present teacher and this leaves the Author's name open to evolutionary changes that oral tradition is open to.

Translating a Pythagorean Greek text into ancient Persian would give a rendering very close to what we call Sanskrit. Vedic Sanskrit has the /r/ sound but this often changes to /l/ in Classical Sanskrit. Neither form of Sanskrit has the theta sound. Patanjali is only available in the Classical Sanskrit.

It seems that there is a substantial probability that the name 'Patanjali' is a phonetic transition of the name 'Pythagoras'. This probability increases with close inspection of the content of the Sutras. The following arguments suggest that stripped of the later Sanskrit notes and commentaries, the *Yoga Sutras* of Patanjali represent a rendering of one of the lost Pythagorean scriptures.

Pythagoras (c582-500 B.C.). Pythagoras is referenced in several works of his contemporaries or near contemporaries. Xenophanes (born c570 B.C.) satirized the Pythagorean belief in transmigration of souls; in one of his (poetic) plays he portrays Pythagoras recognizing the spirit of a dead friend in a dog that is being beaten.

Until now, no complete text from Pythagorean literature before the time of Plato has been found. To date what

we knew of his philosophy and his life was through frag-
ments left from his disciples and other authors. Aristotle
teaches us that his contemporary Pythagoreans were divided, some teaching one thing and some another. Unless
Aristotle was initiated into the esoteric phase he would only
have access to the exoteric schools.

The Pythagoreans contrasted order and disorder in
the terms Cosmos and Chaos, the Apollinian and the Dio-
nysian. Their preference was Apollo, the guardian of order
and moderation. Dionysius was the god of disorder and
immoderation. Pythagoreans claim that Pythagoras was the
first to call the world Cosmos, "from its inherent order."
Thus for the Pythagoreans the Universal Soul is also a
Cosmos. This Cosmos is an ordered unity, immortal, and
divine; a person is divided into a body that is mortal, and a
soul that is not mortal. The soul is a fragment of the divine,
a part of the Universal Soul that animates a mortal body. If
this divine fragment identifies with the body it inhabits,
then it is contaminated by the body. This identification is
an obstruction that confines the soul to the body. This
places the soul in an apparent state of withdrawal from the
Universal Soul. If the soul is contaminated in this way, then
after the death of its body it must continue in this defective
state through cycles of transmigration to cultivate and purify it for gaining a full recollection of its Communion with
the Universal Soul. These notions show a kinship with the
beliefs revealed in the *Yoga Sutras* of Patanjali.

Basic Practices of Pythagoras
1. Obedience.
2. Frequent self-examination.
3. Silence.
4. Periods of fasting.
5. Abstention from eating flesh.
6. Abstention from beans.

7. Plain attirement and modest possessions.

Pythagorean Silence. In the works of authors who cite Pythagoras, there are references to the practice of silence, today referred to as the "Pythagorean Silence." The nature of this Silence and how it is used were mysteries to outsiders.

Self-examination. Socrates is recorded as saying, "The unexamined life is not worth living." This is consistent with the Pythagoreans who required frequent self-examination.

Abstention from Eating Flesh. To the outsider the simplistic abstention from flesh eating seems consistent with the transmigration of souls, but not all Pythagoreans are vegetarians. Pythagoreans do not believe that every animal is sentient though they believe that every living thing is couched in the Universal Soul. Pythagoras is said to have recommended eating meat to his group members who competed in athletics.

Abstention from Beans. The abstention from beans likely refers to fava beans. Universal abstention from fava beans no longer has a rationale. Today we know why they were even forbidden to enter a field of these beans, and this suggests that Pythagoras or people he knew were color-blind.

> **Note: The Fava Bean Story**. The fava bean has a long history in the agriculture of Italy. It is farmed there today and it was farmed there in the time of Pythagoras. Recently it was discovered that this bean has a malicious effect on people who are color-blind. Even its pollen weakens them, makes them sleepy, they faint, and in some cases it functions as an outright poison. Little wonder that the bean was forbidden. It is said that Pythagoras was chased to the border of a (fava) bean field and refused to enter. He was captured.

Patanjali (dates unknown). Patanjali yoga Practice aims at attaining an awake state in which ordinary mental activities, such as will, imagination, belief, and perception are suspended in a form of silence. One could characterize his *Yoga Sutras* as a manual for learning how to shut up. It is a form of self-control.

'Control' is one of the valid English renderings of the Sanskrit term 'yoga'. Indian practitioners call the yoga of Patanjali, Raja Yoga. The Practice of this yoga stops adherence to anything that obstructs the recollection of the Communion between the individual soul and the Universal Soul. This Ceasing to Adhere through the Pythagorean Silence is what is meant by the Pythagoreans to "cultivate and purify" the soul. The recollection of Communion then comes without further effort or desire.

Basic Practices of Patanjali
1. Control.
2. Self-examination.
3. Withdrawal from sense objects (silence).
4. Posture, respiration.
5. Periods of fasting.

Conclusion Summary. If these arguments hold, then when the name 'Pythagoras' was transliterated into a language East of the Indus, his name was rendered finally as 'Patanjali'. This implies that stripped of the later Sanskrit notes and commentaries, the *Yoga Sutras* of Patanjali represent a text from Pythagorean scriptures. Pertinent to this general thesis, we have knowable parallels in the doctrines of Patanjali and Pythagoras.

The Pythagorean role of mathematics for understanding order in the Cosmos is not a concern of the *Yoga Sutras*. The *Timaeus* of Plato is a good introduction for the harmonic ratios. Nicomachus presents a Pythagorean based arithmetic (Britannica Great Books (1952), vol. 11)

These notes on circumstantial historical evidence do not exhaust the possible connections between Pythagoras and Patanjali. Readers are invited to participate in the further search for connections.

End: *Historical Arguments*

Pythagorean Silence
LESSON ONE: Basic Training

INPUT skills

1. Streaming Exercise
2. Closure Concept
3. On the Soul
4. On Individuality
5. Unmodified Experience

LESSON ONE: Basic Training

Introduction: The *streaming exercise* in this lesson is designed to bring you to view your experience without classifications, without bifurcations, i.e., a ceasing to adhere to any *mode* of perception, discernment, or intellectualization. *Intelligibility added from past experience is to be avoided.* Experience without these modalities is named *unmodified experience*. It is possible to apply many modes of partitioning to unmodified experience. At best, the partition modes for unmodified experience can only be *instrumental* guides in our intellectual discourse and daily lives. The instrumental effectiveness for any given partition mode is measured in terms of its utility in rendering our lives more effective to whatever purpose we define.

Streaming Exercise

The nickname for this exercise is the 'dying exercise'. This is based on documented observations reported by people who faced death and survived it. Many recount that under the sensation of imminent death, the entire life they lived passes in review.

Each night, before you go to sleep, you stream your thoughts to repeat the imagery of the day you lived. The exercise is to **recall in a stream of imagery only**. Words and feelings can sidetrack you and interfere with the thought stream. They can constrain what you notice in the imagery. No words are allowed and feelings should be attenuated until they are finally eliminated. The detrimental affect of feelings on the stream of imagery is the bias they introduce. The emphasis remains imagery.

This exercise is easy to describe but usually it is not so easy to do. Some of the problems reported by beginners for this exercise are listed in order of importance as follows:

1. **First** problem: Remember to do the exercise.
2. **Second** problem: Keep the words and feelings out. You will continually insert talk and get distracted by feelings.
3. **Third** problem: Keep to the subject. Your thoughts by association will go off onto one track after another.
4. **Fourth** problem: Do the day in order. Memory without control usually sorts recall according to intensity and continually places episodes out of order. This is the problem of sequence.
5. **Fifth** problem: Keep things connected. The day is usually remembered all chopped up rather than as a holistic presentation.
6. **Sixth** problem: Beginners take too long. If it takes too long, then quit before you finish. The process speeds up with practice. Finally you can finish the exercise in a matter of a few minutes.

Not to discourage you, but to help you accept that the practice is difficult, many people require several years before they can do this exercise properly. If you can master it in less than three years you can consider yourself an exception. Pythagoras required five years of practice before initiation into the esoteric school.

As you might conclude, this exercise impels a *closure* on your entire day. It is likely that when you practice this exercise that you will not live the day quite the same way. You will live it with the sense of responsibility that at the end of the day you must remember the entire day.

One of the side effects of this exercise is that it trains you to put your experience, as you live it, into a connected holistic imagery. This has a remarkable influence on your experience and on how well you remember any sector of experience that follows a sequence, such as reading, etc.

The Illusion of Spontaneity. One of the complaints from beginners in the Streaming Exercise is that in their daily living they experience a loss of spontaneity. This is just a transitional effect. The original basis for measuring spontaneity comes from internalized habituations gained through repetitive practice. In effect, spontaneity is measured in terms of how much our actions differ from those ordained by internalized habits of thought. Therefore, as we go through a new training to replace previous habits, we lose our original basis for judging spontaneity and it seems that spontaneity is lost. Yet as the new habits become more and more internalized, a new basis for interpreting actions as spontaneous is born from the new set of internalized habits.

Closure Concept

Comprehension is a difficult notion to define. One of the more useful concepts for coming to terms with comprehension is the concept of *closure*. Closure can be related to everything that you learn. Exposed to an experience with missing data, using memory, closure presents ways to fill in the missing parts.

To describe closure I shall first take a special example from human visual closure that is connected to verbal ability. Try to see a word in the following pattern:

ЬF ГꞀ ЬP

An answer is given as the last word in this section. If you found a solution to this problem, then you found a closure. It requires your visual and verbal learning to interpolate the missing parts or even to judge that parts are missing.

Another example from visual imagery is found in dot matrix images. It is possible to construct a visual image using only dots of various sizes. A newspaper photo is printed with such dots. If we recognize the image without ambiguity we can ask just how many dots can be randomly removed before we lose the recognition. We can reverse this question and ask, how many randomly printed dots are required before we can recognize an unambiguous image. And furthermore, if we keep filling in the dots we may ask, is this an intensification of our recognition of the image or does it bring about a shift to some other interpretation. Such a shift suggests that the first interpretation could be a case of precipitous judgment, a mistake. For a misinterpretation our only consolation would be if we could rightly claim that we did the best that we could at the time.

Though the dots in themselves have no intrinsic visual force, even when they are arranged randomly on a planar field it may be possible for us to see images. There are random arrays on which we can project an organization even where none was intended. This is much like seeing faces and animals, etc., in a cloud formation.

If we see an unambiguous image and its dots are being randomly removed, we may be able to recognize the intended image in a sparser presentation then if we had to 'construct' the image from zero. Our preview can aid interpretation even at a sparseness where otherwise ambiguity would allow a shift to some other supposed image.

Habituation can aid closure, but it can also bias closure. That habituation can bias closure interpretations even of fully presented images is readily demonstrated with three face photographs of the same person, one frowning, one smiling, and one straight. If you look at the frowning face and then at the straight face you likely will see a slight frowning. If you look at the smiling face and then at the straight face you likely will see a slight smiling. This mode of biased interpretation falls under the general subject of projective psychology.

Closure is a kind of filling in of the gaps, seeing 'wholly' where the display received is only partial. Most of our interpretations are based on partial displays or partial receptions. When we listen to someone speak at a normal rate we can only discern the major phonemes that function as signals that allow us to identify the word or phrase. If you doubt this, ask someone who speaks a language foreign to you to utter even a short sentence in their language. It is likely that you will find you cannot repeat it. It takes many repetitions to internalize a language that is new to you. If someone speaks to you in your own language but uses a word not familiar to you, it is likely you will ask the person to repeat it; you do not have yet the fluency of habituation to hear it correctly.

From a partial display, habituation may lead us to attribute an organization that 'completes' the partial display, connects the parts into a whole. This may correspond well to the way things are, or it may be only a fantasy that leads to false conclusions.

It also provides us with our most sophisticated form of lying. By a careful selection of data we can make true statements that lead people to false closures. This form of lying relies not only on what we neglect to say, but on what we select to say. This sort of closure can be understood in very general terms with common habituation. We have all likely had a series of events occur that led us to an interpretation that later proved wrong. Many great playwrights display these reversals in their plays. Pirandello probably developed these reversals of interpretation further than any other playwright of the 20th Century. Our capacity to appreciate these reversals in artificial display is enhanced by our own exposure to them.

Frequent exposure to such reversals can make one more wary in forming interpretive conclusions.

Verbal Closure. The following example of closure in typing ability can also be used as a paradigm for listening, talking, and reading. When you first learn to type you type by the letter and think each letter. Your typing speed at this stage is very slow. But soon you do not think of the letters, you just seem to find them. This gives you a typing speed of around 20 words per minute. But you begin to type whole words at a time without thinking of the individual letters. When you can do this, mixed with some phrases that you can type without even thinking of the words, then your speed can go to about 45 words per minute. When you can finally type many whole phrases without thinking of the individual words or letters, then your speed exceeds 60 words per minute. What is happening is that you are advancing through different levels of closure. The first level of closure is just remembering the keyboard. The second level is remembering a series of letters for words. Then it increases again when you remember many short series of words automatically. Individual letters close into a whole word and words close into phrases. Phrases and words can close to entire sentences. And so on.

When we talk to each other we must always have use of the closures that we have learned. People learning foreign languages realize the effort required to develop the closures to a sufficiently high level to communicate with a native speaker at natural speeds. It takes a lot of work. But the work aims at forming closures so that we can not only produce sounds at a rapid rate, we can dereference them at a rapid rate. We have to habituate ourselves to the sound sequences so that we do not need to hear every moment in the sequence to grasp words, phrases, etc.

If you read a book that recites an environment familiar to you, then you readily expect rapid fuller comprehension than from reading a work that demands many new closures. This use of familiarity for rapid comprehension also works for the more general presentations of experience.

In the background of efficient comprehension are the thought skills which in a certain sense fall into patterns like riverbeds. The streams of thought as they occurred from early youth establish a specification in how you structure the data into information. These structures can be imposed on new information and consist of the closures that you have established over many years of learning. The possibility of bias generates from past habits. These established patterns can be relentless. It is difficult to change riverbeds.

These riverbeds for the streams of thought are useful in situations that require the rapid flows of habit. It is efficient to know that 7 times 8 is 56 without having to use the higher faculties of thought every time you want to use this result. It is better to drive a car with fast automatic responses rather than with the plodding required to think about every move that you have to make. And it is reasonable to assume that automatic typing is the most efficient. Habit has its virtue.

The virtue in good habits is that you can operate with greater efficiency. But the virtue has a defect. The defect is that information structures may be somewhat deformed by pre-existing patterns for receiving the data. Therefore you may derive information that may have differences that go unnoticed as different. At least these differences will go unnoticed until they become significant to your life somehow.

So the riverbeds of thought may function like blinders that disallow the notice appropriate to certain factors and thus you may be caught by surprise. To help develop ways out of this defective aspect of closure and to help new closures form more readily, the Streaming Exercise is especially useful.

Closure is an old subject and its origins and pristine form in Occidental culture can be found related in the Socratic dialogues of Plato.

In the first half of the 20th century the Gestalt psychologists used closure as a central notion of their psychology. The result of closure was called a 'Gestalt', a German word for 'shape' or 'form'. They applied this term particularly to the solutions of animals placed in problem solving situations. Köhler's book, *Gestalt Psychology*, often speaks of the "subject" and the "objective." He never mentions that they are chimpanzees and bananas (inferenced from his photo illustrations).

Comprehending a text requires closure. We close letters into words and words into phrases, etc. All the notions expressed in a string of words must somehow be comprehended holistically. In general, comprehension is always linked to closure.

An answer to the closure problem: BETTER.

On the Soul

The Soul-Body Problem. Many philosophers speak of the Mind-Body or Soul-Body Problem. The wide promulgation of this 'problem' goes back to the Pythagoreans who do not present it as a problem, but rather as a solution. For Pythagoreans there is an immortal Universal Soul and each individual soul forms a part of this Universal Soul. By conceiving sentient beings as particular souls and regarding the individual soul as a particular expression of the Universal Soul, the individual soul is credited with a form of immortality. This presents the soul as something that can live beyond the life of the body. Furthermore, for practitioners, this indicates a dereference for an out-of-body experience, or if the body dies then it provides a rationale for the transmigration or reincarnation of the soul. For many Christians it gives a rationale for the belief in a judgment day where it is decided whether you are going to heaven or going to hell, etc.

Suffering is an interpretation that relates to the thresholds of our senses. No matter which sense or behavior we speak of, exposure to any extreme can cause pain to us. As for suffering being 'good' or 'bad' for us, only thinking brings us to a judgment. Our own feelings just class the suffering in degrees of pain. Often we do not know at the time of its occurrence whether it is doing us any good or not. We only know if we like it or do not like it. The Pythagoreans knew this very well.

The Pythagoreans believe that when a person is born that as they mature they usually need help to recollect their connection with the Universal Soul. To facilitate this they dug deep shafts where they could practice a form of sensory deprivation. This, combined with stopping thoughts, left nothing but the sense of their own consciousness, which left them with no distractions from recollecting their Communion with the Universal Soul. The preparation for this recollection came to be known as the Pythagorean Silence. In effect, this preparation teaches us how to shut up. This shutting up is portrayed in more detail in the Yoga Sutras in Lesson 5.

The Soul as Motive Force. If we decide that the soul is a motive force for sentient life we have another decision to make; how is this motive force determined? Does each sentient life form possess an individual soul or is it that there is one holistic soul that gets expressed through a variety of individuals. The answer to this question decides whether the soul is to be regarded as internal or external to the life form through which it gets expressed.

In general, many Christians believe that at death their souls leave their body and can exist independently of the body. Many of them also hold the belief that if these souls have not accepted Jesus as their Savior that they remain responsible for their 'sins' and this is used as a motive for conversion to Christianity. The converted believe that Jesus "died for our sins." Among the more primitive Christian believers, death is the doorway to Judgment Day and it is decided on that day whether the soul goes to Heaven or to

Hell. If Jesus is not accepted as Savior, then going to Hell after death becomes in their view a certainty.

A major contradiction arises here because logic tells us that if a soul could be sent to Hell, this would strengthen Hell. The Biblic myth teaches us that Satan was called Lucifer when second to God. He warred against God, lost, and was cast into Hell as a fallen angel. But sending souls to Hell enlarges Satan's army. If the Christian believes that the soul is punished by Satan, this is an affirmation that Satan is performing a service to God. Yet Satan is portrayed as hating God and therefore why should he perform anything that even looks like a service to God. The best thing Satan could do to defy God is reward that soul and do whatever could be done to render that soul happy.

Hell is mentioned 54 times in the Judeo-Christian Bible. To more philosophical Christian believers, Heaven and Hell are states of mind and at death these states of mind get self-imposed according to a supposed degree of guilt. Today there are many different Christian sects and among them we find many notions and details for their Heavens and Hells in terms of descriptions and requirements. Evangelical churches nurture a poetic license into many rhapsodies intended as descriptions of their Hell and Hell's punishment.

> **Note:** Perhaps the most original portrayal of Hell and its punishments is found in Dante's *Inferno*. None of the denizens of Hell have any apparent influence from Satan. Satan is portrayed as a giant in the center of Hell with his feet frozen in a lake of ice. Dante's originality on this subject does not seem to correspond to any beliefs of his time other than Hell is a punishment.

In Christian doctrine there are sects where it is popular to prefer the independent individuality of the soul, which in a sense can be regarded as a form of isolation one from another, which here is to say that the soul is internal to a life form with no necessary external connections. If there is a connection made between souls, it is by choice or chance contingent on compatibility. When this compatibility has a high level between a couple they may come to believe they are 'soul-mates' made one for the other. Can the soul have an existence independent of the body?

The Pythagorean belief is that there is a Universal Soul that gets expressed through every sentient life form. Every sentient life form has an individuality and this individuality couched in the Universal Soul gets expressed as an individual soul. This renders a foundational non-separation for all individual souls. In the original Pythagorean conception, infinity includes everything and therefore it includes the good and the bad. The Yoga Sutras teach us how unmodified experience liberates us from seeing the Universe around us in terms of such simplistic bifurcations and other modifications.

Pythagoreans and Christians. Many of the first Gentile converts to Christianity were Pythagoreans. Despite differences, Christians and Pythagoreans have strong beliefs in common. Men and women are regarded as equals. Jesus held to this even though it was a revolutionary belief to the solidly patriarchal Jews of the time.

> **Note:** After the Exodus the patriarchal Jewish culture under Moses adopted monotheism and their God was a Patriarch referenced as 'Him' or as 'He'. The Pythagorean Universal Soul is without gender.

For the Pythagoreans a woman or a man could be a spiritual leader. It was Pythagoras who introduced this notion of spiritual equality to the Greeks in the 6th Century B.C.

The Pythagoreans were the first to establish mixed gender retreats for spiritual exercises. These retreats were to help the participants gain spiritual strength to better face the exigencies of life. This strength was gained through obtaining the preparatory state that removes any obstacles to the recollection of the Communion of the individual soul with the Universal Soul. This preparatory state is known as the Pythagorean Silence. Once the Pythagorean Silence is achieved the Communion follows without effort or desire.

The Pythagorean retreats inspired Christians to create monasteries and convents, though in this Christian separation of men and women we have rather an apartheid equality. This apartheid equality was likely brought about under the influence of the remaining Christian Disciples. This includes Peter who is credited with the founding of the Roman Catholic Church even though it was Paul who was the first to convert Romans to Christianity. It is likely because of Peter's conservative patriarchal views that the Catholic Church had a long career of only celibate male priests in contradiction to the original Christian doctrine of equality.

When confronting the non-Pythagorean Gentiles, as there seemed no way of offering an immediate tangible reward, the evangelists put the emphasis on living life in a manner that would be rewarded in heaven. This took on a look of salesmanship in offering an after-life-is-over future reward that gave nothing but hope. Even so, this promise was a kind of reward in the peace of mind gained through the assurance of a better after-life. Later the Roman Catholic Church abused this hope through coercive persuasion to purchase Indulgences, in part for the promise to escape hell-fire or to escape the Inquisition. These customs inspired the Lutheran Reformation and began to die out when Pope Leo X (16th Century) died.

NOTE: Pope Innocent III in the 13th Century assigned the Dominicans to start the Inquisition, a form of terrorism. Thousands were tortured and burned alive, accused of heresy. This terrorism became so large in scope the Franciscan order was drafted to help in it. It continued on into the 16th Century under Pope Leo X (a Medici) who strongly supported this depraving of Christian doctrine. (Official elimination was not until the 19th Century.)

For the Pythagoreans, the exercises designed to ac-
quire the required ability to achieve the Pythagorean Silence led to a reward that could be gained within one's current life, the recollection of Communion of the individual
soul with the Universal Soul and the benefit that this gains.
With this gain of spiritual strength and insight they could
better face the exigencies of their current life. In other
words it empowers their sense of well-being in the life they
are now living.

This application of spiritual empowerment to improve the life you now are living is counter to sequestered
religious communities and the naive Christian offer that
you will be rewarded for a good life after you are dead.

For Pythagoreans the quieting in the Pythagorean Silence renders the Communion with the Universal Soul, the
Ultimate Power, vivid and complete. The Pythagorean
could re-enter worldly life with this Communion and the
confidence that it instills.

On Individuality

There are yogi pundits that teach us that if we raise our
awareness of self to a sufficient degree that the sense of self
melts into the universal self and our notion of individual
self fades to nothing. The basis for the individual self,
according to them, is only a delusion. This is not the
Pythagorean view.

Purposely attempting to lose the sense of the
individual self is a form of suicide. The Pythagoreans reject
this view because their practices and methods are not
intended to annihilate our individual existence. Neither are
these methods designed to avoid the exigencies of life. It is
rather a mode of strengthening us as individuals-in-an-
environment so that we not only can better face the

exigencies of life, we can expand our celebration of life. They bring a wanted intensity of feeling and thought. *This Pythagorean intensification of feeling and thought lit the genius that was Ancient Greece.*

On the Wheel of Life. In its present state, the Hindu religion expressly disdains the Wheel of Life. The Hindus agree with the forms of Buddhism, Yoga, and other religions that preach that the Wheel of Life is something to escape and reincarnation is not wanted. In contrast to this Eastern world-view, the Western world wants to celebrate the Wheel of Life and if death remains a necessity then reincarnation would be something that is wanted.

For those who wish to *escape* the Wheel of Life, history has no importance. It merely recapitulates episodes from the Wheel of Life. For those who celebrate the Wheel of Life, history is part of the celebration.

For those who wish to escape the Wheel of Life, enlightenment leads to the destruction of individuality through its absorption into (Union with) the Universal Soul. In effect, individuality has no importance. For those who wish to celebrate the Wheel of Life, individuality is important.

Mechanical existence is a form of sleep-walking. When the Pythagoreans speak of Liberation from the Wheel of Life they are not speaking of death or disrespect for life, nor are they speaking of escape. They are referring to an awakening from unconscious living that mechanical existence is heir to. For example, in our use of language we require mechanical habits for fluency, but we do not want these habits to control us, we want to control these habits and use them as tools for communication. It changes our relationship from automaton where that mechanical existence controls us to one where we can claim responsibility for our actions.

For Pythagoreans, individuality in Communion with the Universal Soul is a wanted state of enlightenment, and individuality remains important.

These contrasts merely indicate the predominant driver attitudes in the Eastern and Western notions of individuality. As with any crowd of individual sentient beings we find a variety of attitudes and these attitudes may include individuals who live in contradiction to the prevailing attitudes of their region.

In Lesson 5, the Yoga Sutras reveal how to achieve the Pythagorean Silence required for the recollection of Communion.

Unmodified Experience

1. Unmodified experience for the individual is experience taken without any of its possible partitions, i.e., without words, without classifications, without concepts, without intellectual projections, without emotional projections, i.e., no assigned modalities.
2. The Streaming Exercise develops the power to re-establish and to hold your awareness of unmodified experience.
3. This submersion into unmodified experience renders awareness of our modes of thought and releases us from their hold on us.
4. This release from modes of thought is a ceasing to adhere.
5. Some pundits misname this ceasing to adhere as 'detachment'.
6. Detachment has the connotation of not caring about it.
7. Not caring is not human.
8. Ceasing to adhere does not imply that you do not care about it; it implies that you have come to know that modalities derived from experience are functionally independent of your selfhood.
9. Ceasing to adhere to a particular modality allows you to explore other modalities and opens the way to creating new modalities.

10. This power to re-establish and to hold your awareness of un-modified experience opens the way to the Pythagorean Silence.

Identification

1. Identification and Identity are different in kind.
2. Identity is the 'I am' *with* all its modalities.
3. Identification is the name for adherence to modalities.
4. Identification with modalities forgets 'I am'.
5. Ceasing to adhere to modalities releases 'I am' from identification.

END: *Lesson One*

Pythagorean Silence
LESSON TWO: Remembering

STAYPUT, the problem of retention

1. Tesla Exercise
2. Retention
   a. Recognition
   b. Recollection
   c. Recall
3. Interrogation
   Apodeictic Fictions
   Data-Field Testing
   Field-Free Determinations
4. Doings and Happenings
5. Transcending the Individual Self

LESSON TWO: Remembering

Introduction: The *Tesla exercise* in this lesson is designed to bring you to view your experience selectively. This form of Recollection is associated with selections from your autobiography. It is the act of localizing through time, with more or less precision, the source of an occasion in your life. At first this sort of remembering can be quite vague. Persistence brings focus and focus brings precision.

The unexamined life is not worth living.

This dictum was taught by Socrates as recorded in Plato's Dialogues (Athens c400 B.C.). It is one of the key dictums of the Pythagorean Schools and in those schools it is treated as a command. It associates with the Delphi Oracle dictum over the entry gate, "Know your self."

One of the uses of the Streaming Exercise (Dying Exercise) is to put events in temporal sequence. Even though the Streaming Exercise puts the daily events in their time sequence this is not really a recollection. Recollection entails selection. The Tesla Exercise is a form of *recollec-*

tion. Tesla describes the exercise for recollection that he derived as a solution to a personal affliction.

Tesla Exercise

Nikola Tesla (1856—1943), in an essay entitled "The Problem of Increasing Human Energy" (1900), wrote about an exercise that became a necessity for him. He states,

"A long time ago, when I was a boy, I was afflicted with a singular trouble, which seems to have been due to an extraordinary excitability of the retina. It was the appearance of images which, by their persistence, marred the vision of real objects and interfered with thought. When a word was said to me, the image of the object which it designated would appear vividly before my eyes, and many times it was impossible for me to tell whether the object I saw was real or not. This caused me great discomfort and anxiety, and I tried hard to free myself of the spell. But for a long time I tried in vain, and it was not, as I still clearly recollect, until I was about twelve years old that I succeeded for the first time, by an effort of the will, in banishing an image which presented itself. My happiness will never be as complete as it was then, but, unfortunately (as I thought at that time), the old trouble returned, and with it my anxiety. Here it was that the observations to which I refer began. I noted, namely, that whenever the image of an object appeared before my eyes I had seen something which reminded me of it. In the first instances I thought this to be purely accidental, but soon I convinced myself that it was not so. A visual impression, consciously or unconsciously received, invariably preceded the appearance of the image. Gradually the desire arose in me to find out, every time, what caused the images to appear, and the satisfaction of this desire soon became a necessity. The next observation I made was that, just as these images followed as a result of something I had seen, so also the thoughts which I conceived were suggested in like manner. Again, I experienced the same desire to locate the image which caused the thought, and this search for the visual impression soon grew to be a second nature. My mind became automatic, as it were, and in the course of years of continued almost unconscious performance, I acquired the ability of locating every time and, as a rule, instantly the visual impression which started the thought. Nor is this all. It was not long before I was aware that also all my movements were prompted in the same way, and so, searching, observing, and verifying continuously, year after year, I have, by every thought and every act of mine, demonstrated, and do so daily, to my absolute satisfaction, that I am an automaton endowed with power of movement, which merely responds to external stimuli beating upon my sense organs, and thinks and acts and moves accordingly. I remember only one or two cases in all my life in which I was unable to locate the first impression which prompted a movement or a thought, or even a dream."

Regardless of whether you accept or reject Tesla's conclusion that he is an automaton, this exercise is a logical extension of the Streaming Exercise, but with some important differences:

1. You begin at the result and trace backwards.

2. This trace is selective for the series of events relevant to the result.
3. This series is not necessarily continuous since you only choose the relevant events.
4. Words and feelings are not forbidden when they play a guiding role in determining relevance.

Much of Tesla's enormous concentration power and creative ability derived from this extraordinary recollection exercise. The Streaming Exercise is predominantly an exercise in *recall* (without words, etc.). The Tesla Exercise is predominantly an exercise in *recollection* (tracing relevance back through time). Both exercises are very difficult in the beginning. It is as if human thought does not like protracted restrictions or systematic control.

Historical Note: Nikola Tesla was involved with the invention of every major device used by the American electric companies and now by electric companies the world over. His dream was to transmit electricity without wires and have it generated by unconsumed resources. His generators were the first used anywhere that run only by natural resources that are not consumed (the Niagara Falls electricity generating plant, etc.). He would *not* have approved of using atomic energy for generating electricity because this is a fuel that is consumed. His ecosystem thinking would likely have rejected this use for other reasons as well. The system of alternating current (AC) used in the world today is based on Tesla's work.

In 1943, the U.S. Supreme Court removed the radio patents of Marconi in view of the fact that not only was Marconi familiar with the work of Tesla (a great source of ideas), but Tesla had already tested and patented the radio devices (but with no fanfare). He also constructed the first radio controlled device, a model boat (patented 8 November 1898). He was twice recommended for the Nobel Prize but it was never offered to him. Marconi won the Nobel Prize for patents that are no longer his.

Tesla had come to America to work for Edison. Edison argued for direct current and Tesla argued for alternating current. Tesla left Edison and became sponsored by Westinghouse. Edison lost the argument for direct current and admitted later in his life that the position he had held against alternating current was one of the most important mistakes of his life.

Retention

    A. Memory.
    B. Remembering.
        1. Recognition.
        2. Recollection.
        3. Recall.

A. Memory. Much study has been made on memory. There is a long history concerning how to improve memory. This history goes back more than three thousand years. Memory is the database that holds whatever we have learned. The main characteristic of memory is the use of data structures that catalog our memories associatively or holistically, etc. These structures tend to be fairly static or dynamic according to the variety and intensity of the ongoing personal experience.

One of the most common methods for improving memory is the development of mnemonic devices. In ancient Greece the orators trained by first putting a building into their memories. This building was actually walked around and through room by room systematically and always in the same order to memorize the building and its rooms with all their characteristics. Then when a speech was to be learned the orator furnished and decorated the memory of this building with the speech. Then as the speech is given it is remembered by walking mentally through and around this building and reciting the furnishings and decorations that were placed there. This building is the mnemonic device.

There are many sorts of mnemonic devices. There are many books on memory suggesting how to develop and to use mnemonic devices. If you are interested in developing the use of mnemonic devices you should consult the growing literature on this subject.

B. Remembering. To remember is to retrieve from memory and of course this implies *access* to memory. The following terms designate three modes of retrieval from memory:

      1. Recognition.
      2. Recollection.
      3. Recall.

If you look these terms up in a dictionary, they look like synonyms. Memory specialists have proposed finer distinctions to make conversing about retrieval from memory more precise and they take fuller advantage of the different words available. Registering, learning, memory, and remembering form an interrelated foursome. Registering is INPUT, learning is THRUPUT, memory is STAYPUT, remembering is OUTPUT (even if you are remembering without speaking, etc.).

1. Recognition is the foundation for all present experience. If you had no retention of past experiences, the present would be completely unintelligible to you. You would recognize nothing in terms of your past experience. Recognition is the passive recall of past experience as it applies to the present. The richness of our past experience can help us interpret a present experience. It can also lead us astray.

> **Note:** Experiencing without the imposition of past experience for intelligibility is said to be experience unmodified by past experience. Experience unmodified by past experience excludes recognition.

Recognition in reading is passive. This notion of passive indicates that the stimulus for recognition is external to you. It is the seeing combined with retained experience that allows the recognition to occur. In testing, multiple choice questions play heavily on our capacity to recognize. In another way, true-false tests play on this capacity to recognize from our past experience. As you read you are registering and dereferencing. The dereferencing requires that you recognize what you see. When successful, this recognition is generally passive. When it fails, we have to recollect, or look it up, or decide to ignore it.

One set of experiments concerning recognition and orientation is called the **sensory deprivation experiments**. They were done at Stanford University, etc. The human subject was put into a rubber suit with breathing tubes, fed intravenously, ears blocked; eyes blocked, and put in a tank of water so that there was no particular sense of weight or direction. Excretions were handled better than in the first American spacesuits, where it was a forgotten problem. Deprived of these senses the subjects lost their orientation in a surprisingly short time (two or three days). When they came out of the tanks they could not articulate well. They were also in a high state of suggestibility. If you told one to go jump in the lake (s)he might well start looking for a lake. Language recognition remains relatively intact. But the subjects required a reorientation period before their behavior could be regarded as normal. I have yet to find any documentation suggesting permanent damage to subjects of these experiments, nor have I heard of any lawsuits associated with them, but institutions now seem to have a fear of this research. (This research is now expressly forbidden at Stanford and some other institutions.)

These experimental results could be interpreted as showing that our immediate environment is our most important mnemonic device. It also could be argued that *remembering through recognition is the basis for maintaining human orientation.*

2. Recollection here is defined as a localization in the personal past. The Tesla Exercise is a form of recollection where you start with a result and trace back through time the series of events that led to the result you are examining. This allows the construction of the historical context of this result.

> **Note:** Though the moment you become aware of Communion through recollection can be placed in time, Communion itself is independent of time.

If your remembering requires putting together the historical context of an event in your life from previous impressions without adding anything to these impressions, then you are recollecting. Recollection is associated with your autobiography. It is the act of localizing in time, with more or less precision, a past occasion of your life. This sort of remembering can also be quite vague. You may only have a vague notion that you have experienced a certain occasion or not. When you search for the origins for a result that you are examining, in effect, you are searching for the first significant stimulus that started the series that led to that result. Recollection is not merely the recalling of an autobiographical fact. It requires placing it in time. When recollecting you also have the sensation of reliving the feelings of the occasions.

Very young children have not yet developed a clear sense of time. Young children and archaic cultures use a kind of time that can be characterized as *intensity*. If a kid falls down with a lollipop in mouth and the lollipop gets rammed up the throat, it is an occasion that is remembered. Other occasions can then be placed before the 'lollipop' or after the 'lollipop', etc.

3. Recall is a form of retrieval associated with experience and storytelling. It differs from Recollection in that Recollection is looking for the source or origin of a thought or motivation, Recall is episodic and can be expressed as a continuous stream of imagery or words or multimedia. The stories we tell to each other about things we have seen, heard, or that have happened to us are episodic.

Recall from reading is a construction from reading. It requires an interaction of activities that is directed toward representing the memory of a text. It can be oral or written or in imagery streamed in your head, etc. Each person has a richness of experience that cannot be identical with another person's experience. This variation in experience gives each of us the particular dispositions that form our character. One of the consequences of these differences is that each person has a personal way of recalling, a personal way of constructing a recall.

Intelligibility to others depends on how public you can render personal recall. This can be enhanced with images, videos, tone of voice, acting out, etc.

> **Note:** This personal way of constructing recall stems from our attempts to render the episode intelligible to others. This is quite different from the Dying Exercise, which remains personal and *intelligibility added from past experience is to be avoided.*

Many people who have shared some experience in the past find later that their memories of the occasion do not always match. Even where their conclusions seem to match they may differ in the way they came to these conclusions.

Regardless of the differences that may lie behind the construction of a recall there is a common result when recalls are practiced. The more often you recall a certain text or episode in your life the easier and the more rapid becomes the recall. You learn the particular recall with more economy of time and effort and you may pick up more detail. Furthermore, it develops economy of time and effort in the general technique of recall.

Interrogation

Introduction. Modes of interrogation influence how we face our daily experience. This in turn influences how we remember experience. The following three role categories, in popular use among social anthropologists, determine very different modes of interrogation:

> **Participants:** Insider members of the society, who internalize the habitual modes of thought through a thorough apprenticeship.
>
> **Observers:** Outsiders who have little or no apprenticeship for internalizing the habitual modes of thought of the visited society.
>
> **Participant-Observers:** Are outsider-insider members of the society that live in the hyphen of immanent reversibility, an adherence through apprenticeship, a non-adherence through interrogation.

> Note: These categories have a fuzzy separation but are useful as reference terms as dominant modes of awareness of ourselves in our milieu. In a later context these roles are applied to character types (Personal Interfaces: Lesson 4).

In general, well-conditioned **insiders** do not question custom or law unless it is to assure that they themselves are conforming within the latitude allowed by custom or law. The arbitrariness of social conventions used in their reasoning is rendered invisible to them through habituation or trained denial. If behavior criticism exists, it targets non-conformity and uses sanctions to render conformation.

A person who 'knows' that if they do not get baptized that they will go to hell when they die may be respecting a long well-defined family tradition. As an insider (s)he does not have the perspective required to test the arbitrariness of this act. (S)he well 'knows' that testing it could have dire consequences.

As an **outsider** one may readily note the differences from one's own beliefs and practices. At the same time there is a possible blindness to the systems of emotions and values of the foreign society, the very drivers of behavior for that society. The outsider comes from another point of view. Even outsiders willing to adapt to a foreign society do so usually with an accent. As an outsider, one may never fully understand the 'grammar' of behavior in the way required to live it without accent. Whatever the degree of accent, fluency requires internalization.

Perhaps a non-gullible outsider comes to know about the local belief concerning baptism. This outsider may become confused, or may decide that it is a useless act, or may be glad that (s)he found out in time. A recognition of choices can impose interrogation onto the observing outsider whether it is wanted or not.

The **participant-observer** is in a state of immanent reversibility, an adherence developed through apprenticeship and a non-adherence obtained through interrogation. This state is regarded as the most effective for students and travelers who want to understand other cultures.

It is through interrogation that the drivers of behavior are rendered more visible. This discussion implies that habits and customs drive our actions and influence what we pay attention to and what we neglect. These internalized drivers are the architects of our reference-frames that we use for defining our world-view. The discussion also suggests that interrogation can help us cease adherence to these internalized conventional principles and beliefs. We become more open to seeing factors significant to a foreign culture that have a different significance from our own, a useful trait for travelers.

Apodeictic Fictions. When we use categories that are artificially constructed but useful in argument, such as {participant, observer, participant-observer}, we are using *apodeictic constructs*. These constructs are used in arguments to exhibit principles or give proof. This use in argument is apodeictic, keeping close to the original Greek, 'ἀποδειξις', 'a setting forth', 'arguments in proof of''. Apodeictic *constructs* are known to be artificial. Apodeictic *conventions* may or may not be known to be artificial. Furthermore, if apodeictic constructs have no dereference to matters-of-fact, they are *apodeictic fictions*.

Data-Field Testing. A reference-frame may have apodeictic usage. Granting an apodeictic reference-frame that makes use of a data-field, we now ask, what is the nature of the relationship between the apodeictic reference-frame and its data-field? A careful consideration requires regarding possible feed-forward/feed-back relations between them. In feed-forward the reference-frame conditions how we access the data-field. Regarding how the reference-frame influences our access to the data-field we consider what to look at, what we look for, what we neglect, etc. In feed-back the data-field can influence the reference-frame. Regarding how the data-field influences the reference-frame we consider modes of disconfirmation, error, and reference-frame tests for robustness. Therefore these condition orders are seen as immanently reversible.

Field-Free Determinations. An apodeictic reference-frame may lead us to new points in the data-field that might not have been regarded without the indications derived from that reference-frame. A classic example is the periodic table of elements developed by Mendeleyev (1834-1907) in 1869. In 1871 he published an improved version that left gaps for elements that were not yet discovered. This led to a systematic search for new elements. Gallium, Germanium, and Scandium were the first predicted elements discovered. In its refined form, the periodic table also provides a model that tells us when to stop looking.

Reference-frames can teach us new ways or places to observe in the data-field. These determinations are called field-free determinations because they first derive from a reference-frame without an immediate regard for the data-field. In a manner of speaking these are field-free truth values and are formal determinations. Should all field-free determinations require data-field testing? The answer for science is yes. All such premises must ultimately dereference to matters-of-fact (selections from the data-field). The answer for formal logic is no. In this sense formal logic is not a science, but its uses for field-free determinations provide a powerful exploration tool for science.

We might ask more particularly how field-free determinations have any significant dereferences. For science this can be characterized as the Problem of Deduction. As yet undiscovered elements were deduced from Mendeleev's periodic table of elements. The truth of the deduction was contingent on discovering the predicted elements. This

Problem of Deduction is as important as the better known Problem of Induction. For Science both are contingent on the data-field. It is in their contingency that we find common ground for these respective problems.

Doings and Happenings

'Spirit' and 'Soul' are interchangeable terms. Both the individual and Universal Soul or Spirit are represented in ancient Greek with the term 'ψυχη' (psyche, English pronounce "sigh-key"). The complete representation of the Universal Soul is in the individual soul and the complete representation of the individual soul is in the Universal Soul. The Communion referred to in Lesson 1 is a discursive mode of presentation. In this discursive mode the individual soul and the Universal Soul are the two aspects of Communion regarded in synchronicity and as coextensive.

Synchronicity = no preference in causal direction;
Coextensive = at the same moment in space.

To help understand the nature of the intertwining of the individual soul and the Universal Soul, think of a holographic image. If we cut it in half we have twin images as complete as the original image. Every piece that we cut contains the complete image of the whole and the whole has the complete image of every cut, no more and no less. This holistic view is indicated when we say that individual sentient beings are created by and create the Universal Soul. It is the dereference for 'cutting' that allows the formation of individuals. However, the Communion of the individual with the Universal Spirit shows us bound together.

There is a danger that our state of Communion may remain blocked by all the environmental noise within us and around us. Therefore, in regard to the memory of all sentient beings, most of us need exercises that unshroud the recollection of the Universal Soul. It is the Communion of ourselves with the Universal Soul that is our *sentient environment*.

All our constructed interface reference-frames are expressed in human terms, therefore by necessity are anthropomorphic. However, when we use these artificial constructs for making sense of our experience they are, by their abstraction, lossy (i.e., entails a loss) representations and therefore by necessity defective. This is also why our constructs that interface with our sentient environment, by necessity, exhibit a defective anthropomorphism

> **NOTE:** Some philosophers believe it is possible to make formulations that are not anthropomorphic. They fail to see the formulator in the formulation.

When we construct reference-frames they must be from our nature not only anthropomorphic, which is always the case, but they are also artificial constructs, which could allow the introduction of construct artifacts that with respect to our sentient environment introduce fictions. This introduction of lossy reference-frames with the possible introduction of fictions disallows claims for objectivity in any of these constructed interfaces. Declaring any artificial interface as objective is preaching a delusion.

Born premature, our premature senses can become intensified to a point that our sensations become distractions from our awareness of the Universal Spirit. This hinders us from achieving the full-awareness of a spiritual state that should be natural to us. The Pythagoreans developed exercises that facilitate achieving this awareness. One of the first goals for these exercises is to quiet any distractions that shroud the Universal Spirit from us. This quieting of distractions leads to what is known as the Pythagorean Silence.

Though in part this Silence is a kind of withdrawal from sensory distractions, a form of sensory deprivation, this is not the goal of this Silence. Exercises are described in this text to facilitate sufficient control to practice what seems at first a kind of withdrawal from these distractions. But as just said, this withdrawal is not the intention. The preparatory state that is wanted is a 'ceasing to adhere'. This state removes any obstacles to our recollection of Communion, and this state can be maintained in daily life as our Sentient Environment.

In bad translations of Sanskrit texts regarding spiritual development, the term 'detachment' is often used. Detachment is presented as a goal for facilitating spiritual development. The connotations of this term have allowed many people to misconstrue this as indicating that they should not care about things or anything. This is completely opposed to human nature, which is a caring nature. To avoid the necessity of a continual correction on this point we use another term in the form of a phrase, a 'Ceasing to Adhere' or 'Ceasing Adherence'. In this text this phrase is first taken in two aspects. One is a ceasing to identify with what you regard as doings; the other is a ceasing to identify with what you regard as happenings. This does not imply that you do not care about these things.

If you identify with what you regard as doings, then you start creating or accepting concepts like 'freedom' and 'free will' as if they had an existence independent of the Sentient Environment. If you identify with what you regard as happenings, then you start creating or accepting concepts like 'chance' and 'determinism' as if they had an existence independent of the Sentient Environment.

> **Note:** In a sense this monadic focus on either 'doings' or 'happenings' is a generalized interpretation of 'what is the sound of one hand clapping'. The sound is in the relation between the two hands. Even so, people with good

reflexes make a joke of this Japanese Zen question by training themselves to clap with one hand.

Ceasing to Adhere to these aspects of how you see your life in terms of Doings-Happenings is to identify with the position of the hyphen and accept your notion of life as the interface between the two extremes. This is also known as the Middle Path or Middle Way. Many Greeks in Plato's time were Pythagoreans and one of the popular dictums of the time was to take the Middle Path, avoid the extremes. It is a kind of stepping stone exercise toward sensing the Sentient Environment with no interface whatsoever. Our Sentient Environment is the Communion of our individual self with the Universal Spirit and it is this Communion that couches our sentient identity.

Transcending the Individual Self

1. From the partitions we make in our unmodified experience we derive a reality that transcends our individual self (our personal universe).
2. This reality is the Universe of happenings, which for the most part we have no personal control over.
3. We confront this Universe of happenings with our personal universe of what we claim that we do.
4. The partitions of doings and happenings stand in opposition to each other and our unmodified experience remains their foundation.
5. Our universe of Doings-Happenings is under a continual feed-forward feed-back of confirmation and testing.
6. The determination of the nature of this confirmation and testing, defines how we transcend the individual self.
7. People who never transcend their individual self remain in the solipsist state partially or fully.
8. The partial solipsist is said to build castles in the sky and the full solipsist is said to build castles in the sky and then lives in them.
9. To maintain the solipsist state requires the denial that there are partitions in our experience that are beyond our control.

10. This lack of control in a partition of unmodified experience may be partial or fully so.
11. Admitting any lack of control in a partition of unmodified experience is the foundation for the individual self to transcend the solipsist state.
12. It is a declaration of a universe that happens to the individual self and admits a reality to other individuals.
13. This happening Universe is the source of constraints on what the individual self can do.
14. That this happening Universe constrains our universe of doing is constantly put to the test.
15. These tests not only help us define the characteristics of these constraints over us, but define the extent of their power over us and the limits of our power over the Universe of happenings.

END: *Lesson Two*

Pythagorean Silence
LESSON THREE: Knowing, Doing, Understanding

THRUPUT, the problem of processing

1. Trobriand Exercise
2. Experience Modifications
    Habitual Thought
    Conventions
    Dereferencing
    Formal Reasoning
    Data-Field
3. What is Truth
    Invariant Truth
    Data-Field Access
4. Transcendental Knowing
    Transcendent Instruments
    Independent Agreement
5. Knowledge and Truth

LESSON THREE: Knowing, Doing, Understanding

Introduction: The *Trobriand exercise* in this lesson is designed to intensify the awareness of connections and associations. Malinowski concluded that the Trobrianders could not see the relation between an apple that is an unripe green and when that apple is ripe and red. This relation of changes through time does not seem to be indicated in the Trobriand culture. Whether or not Malinowski's observation is correct does not matter here. The use of this notion here is to show that even in our own culture we have many experiences that are isolated from each other in time or space only because we ignore or do not know the connections. To counter this ignorance and further increase powers of association the following exercise is recommended.

Trobriand Exercise

This exercise can be done with abstract concepts or individual objects. Begin with a simple manufactured object such as a spoon and imagine its beginning to its present state to its demise. If the spoon is stainless steel you might imagine the iron mines as a beginning. This associates spoons with miners and hard hats, etc. Though you could project this study through the evolution of the Earth for the origins of the iron mine, etc., this knowledge transcends the possibility of direct experience and therefore transcends the purpose of this exercise.

> **Note:** You are advised to limit your associations to the people, situations, and events known to be within the limits of direct human experience. These limits include anything open to direct experience in the creation and the destruction of the object under study.

Projecting into the future we examine the possible demise of the spoon. This could be imagined as a wearing down, or maybe it is remelted for making it into something else. Maybe it will go to powder and become part of the mixture of earth. This is just the beginning of the thinking that is possible on the subject of an ordinary stainless steel spoon.

For the spoon we have yet to consider its designer, the people who manufactured it, the people who manufactured the instruments for manufacturing it, the distributors, the users. We also have yet to consider the smelting of the iron and the processing for steel. It becomes quite involved when we try to consider all the interconnections.

As you can see, a complete consideration of this life of a spoon involves a great extension of information, all of which is within the limits of possible direct experience but much of which is not immediately available to you. This is why you start with something apparently simple.

Once you get in the habit of regarding each object in terms of its interconnections with its past and its future you will not be able to look at any object the same way as before. These interconnections form a closure where the object appears more and more interwoven with the fabric of the civilization that created it.

Try this exercise in regard to a piece of paper (note that not all papers are made from trees).

Experience Modifications

Introduction. Human senses and perception are the input boundaries to human experience. They also provide the means for partitioning the human experience into parts. Artists who learn to produce accurate representations on flat surfaces have taught us that such presentations have no distinct lines or divisions in them. The best we can have are suggestions of lines and divisions. Should the artist actually emphasize these suggested lines and divisions by drawing or painting them with a clarity beyond the actual presentation we then have representation that has what we call *cartoon clarity*. Even in cartoon representations we have what we interpret as lines that suggest continuations that are not actually drawn. A child's drawing of teeth makes each tooth distinct with apparently solid complete lines whereas the trained cartoonist uses lines that only suggest the complete distinction.

It is useful here to introduce some of the effects that perception has on the interpretation of the data we derive from our sensory apparatus. It is in the constructs of perception that we derive a clarity in lines and divisions, which *de facto* do not exist with clarity in the visible presentation. This exaggerated clarity is the first step toward conceptualization. If perceptions are sensory constructs that have a clarity of lines and distinctions that exceed the clarity of the presentation to our senses, then this forming of sensory constructs is the first step toward an abstraction from our experience.

This notion of abstraction is dereferenced as 'a leaving out of sensory data'. To abstract from the presentation is to produce a lossy representation of the presentation. The shadings we sense in the presentation are reduced in a manner that exaggerates the clarity of the suggested lines and distinctions. It is from these abstractions that we derive our concepts and in effect this implies that our concepts often have the fault of cartoon clarity.

Declaring that our concepts are abstractions is consistent with current belief. But abstractions are lossy representations, so how does it come about that lossy representations are used so abundantly and have been found so useful to human communication? As with any construct that we find useful, this usefulness has to be determined within a context in which the construct is used. In the case of human usage this context includes the notion of intent and accomplishment.

There are different possible partition modes for the same field of experience. This fact points to the difficulty in coming to terms with these partitions. That there can be more than one partition mode over the same field of experience directs us to question what is being dereferenced when we use one mode or another mode.

To give an artificial model for coming to terms with modes of partitioning, consider finding ways to locate a point on a plane. In the 7th grade you used Cartesian based coordinates and located a point using the coordinates of x and y that cross each other perpendicular at the coordinates (0,0), called the 'origin'. Using these Cartesian coordinates you can express the location of any given point P as P(x,y). Since any point is expressible as P(x,y) you have a way of naming any point that can be located with Real numbers.

Note: Descartes used only unsigned numbers. Today's Cartesian coordinates have extended his analytic geometry to include signed numbers, etc.

There are other ways of naming every point with numbers. If you take trigonometry you discover that you can define the position of every point that can be located with Real numbers using what are called polar coordinates. Use a horizontal line segment and the origin is placed by convention on the left end. From this left end is a ray connecting to the origin and it can be rotated around this origin. We can choose any length on this ray and say it has a length, r, and the angle, θ, is taken with respect to the reference horizontal line segment. Therefore any point on the plane that can be located with Real numbers is expressible as $P(\theta,r)$. The origin is $r = 0$ at any angle, this is expressible as $(\theta,0)$. Both of these coordinate systems completely map the Euclidean plane but they are distinctly different modes of representation and use very different formulas to represent the various geometric figures of analytic geometry.

In a similar way our unmodified experience is open to many modes of partitioning that can map the details of our experience in different ways. These different modes can generate culture shock to amateur world travelers when they encounter different cultures. The practitioner of unmodified experience has a higher awareness of the scope of possible partitions and therefore is not so affected by culture shock.

Some examples of modified experience: In the case of artists we could have a cartoonist, an impressionist, and a pointillist all painting the same scene. We likely will recognize that they are three distinct representations of the same scene. This can be used as a paradigm for how different people think about the same object. We can carry the paradigm further to include episodic experience. Remember Kurosawa's film *Rashomon*. All the witnesses to a violent event had their own version of it, some contained lies, some were sincere, and their stories vary so much that the truth cannot be determined.

Habitual Thought. The milieu that gives rise to the beliefs one adheres to sinks into a background dimmed by habitual acquaintance. Socrates asserted that the unexamined life is not worth living. It would likely be too strong a claim even for those who reflect on their lives that they found the sources of all the habits of custom and belief that direct their lives.

> **Note:** Tesla remains an example of someone who obtained an extreme degree of source finding, but he never transcended the sense of being an automaton (being mechanical).

As ingrained patterns these habits impel one to prefer one perspective over another possibility. The knowledge and understanding we have of ourselves and the world around us are couched in these habitual modes of thought.

Conventions. A convention refers to any notion determined by agreement, no matter how fuzzy or crisp the determination might be, no matter how tacit or explicit the agreement might be. Such conventions always have a mediate usage. By conventions we use money as a measure of assigned values for goods and services; we use money for exchange of goods and services. This measure is the mediate use for money; money thus mediates exchanges. The more goods and services we obtain with a fixed amount of money, the more value we ascribe to the money. Money itself is a commodity for exchange, but its value remains determined by what a user may purchase and this determination is by a moveable convention. The original usage for conventions remains mediate. Any other use can open the possibility of abuse or a misunderstanding of the basis for conventions (discussed further below in Dereferencing section).

Language conventions, as with all conventions, must be learned. It is somewhat arbitrary which language system be adopted in a community as long as it is sufficiently rich or developable for the requirements of verbal expression. Thus we may speak of a particular language as an arbitrary convention. It is as arbitrary as the dollar system or the euro system.

Eating and drinking are human necessities, how to eat and drink are by conventions that may vary from culture to culture.

Deferencing. When we identify a reference language with the experience it maps, we ignore the mediate requirements for valid language reference. It is like regarding the map as the territory (this problem is a major concern in General Semantics).

With toddler children, when we point to an object with the intention that the child regard that object, the child regards the pointing finger. The sequence of events for fuller comprehension requires two steps:

> 1. Regard the pointing finger,
> 2. Regard the object pointed at.

The first step is the *reference*.
The second step is the *dereference*.

Young children who see the pointing finger generally do not perceive it as a reference intended for dereferencing. It is taken unwittingly as its own reference. This precludes the intentional dereferencing of the finger. As the child learns a reference language, the problem of reference and dereference is fundamental to what the child is learning. Every symbolic representation implies these two aspects. This subject merits more research.

Our language is one of our most elaborate resources for referencing our experience. Our experience, however we hold it, is the field for dereference. The couch for the representation of our experience is memory. This includes our previous experience, our present experience, and our anticipated experience.

In the case of the pointing finger, maturity of judgment requires that we know the sequence of seeing the finger and looking at the object pointed at. In the case of language reference, there are clear instances where something other than dereferencing seems to happen. The possibility of this other something is enhanced by the dependence of dereferencing to remembered experience. Fluency in speech requires considerable dereferencing to memories. This helps speed verbal expression, but this speed can degenerate into a trade-off with accuracy. Even during the course of a day, memory may diminish or amplify the intensity of its holding of original experience. In part this may come from the mnemonic effects of our immediate environment. For some types of experience, these changes can generate trouble causing distortions in the dereference.

A child who unwittingly takes the pointing finger as a self-reference can learn to point a finger without yet understanding what the original intent was. This important lesson is applicable to adult language use. Most adults use many language utterances that cannot be dereferenced to memories of direct experience. In effect, they use words that point to nothing from their direct experience, but they use them as if they did.

If you have been to Larissa and can tell others how to get there, you are a right and good guide. If you have never been to Larissa and can tell others how to get there, you are also a right and good guide, etc.

Formal Reasoning. Formal reasoning is without dereferencing. This is the form of 'thinking' that we can program computers to do. This is the ultimate in formal reasoning. In effect, general purpose computers can compute with formal rules of syntax without dereferencing. There is much current research in computer hardware to extend sensory devices to imitate human sensors. This widens the horizon for computer dereferencing. The great stumbling block for computers is to modify input into a holistic perception, the problem of perceptual closure (see Lesson 1), which the digital computer at best can only simulate. In digital computers, data and information remain monadic (self-contained) and in this sense express important limitations of their creators and their current monadic reasoning methods.

Computer knowledge-based systems were founded on the recognition of the importance of dereferencing. Only a knowledge-based system has the capacity to simulate dereferencing. I say simulate because the current computers can only dereference to second-hand data and information. Even so, much of human 'knowing' is of this second-hand sort. If you are committed to accurate dereferencing, then you hold second-hand information clearly marked as second-hand information until you can make it first-hand.

Using our reasoning independent of dereferencing is, in a manner of speaking, a ceasing to adhere to matters-of-fact, a ceasing to adhere to content. This mode of ceasing to adhere can be useful in coming to terms with our memories (interpretation of the past) and anticipations (formulating future possibilities). Formulating expectations also sets us up for disappointment or fulfillment. Only if we are able to dereference as we go can we claim we are adhering to matters-of-fact or our memory of matters-of-fact. Our ability to re-adhere to matters-of-fact provides a context for our attempts to implement or experience our anticipations.

In effect, a reference-frame provides a mode for **addressing** personal events (matters-of-fact in sensation, perception, or memory). To dereference these events is equivalent to perceiving **what is at the address**. Our general problem with reference-frames is how do we discern what is put into the event by the reference-frame and what is not. The what-is-not is a data-field dereference. The what-is are artifacts from the reference-frame. Are 'God', 'Freedom', and 'Immortality' artifacts born from reference-frames, or can they be dereferenced to the data-field, to matters-of-fact. Most people do not bother to ask. Kant made these questions a central issue in his *Critique of Pure Reason*.

Many educated people use terms that are empty when dereferenced and they talk as if these terms could be dereferenced. In effect, they use terms for which they have no valid address for dereferencing. When we treat such invalid addresses as if valid, we have an address where nobody is home, etc., the attempted dereferencing can end up as much ado about nothing. Faulty dereferencing is a common occurrence.

Many of the problems in human references are directly related to the individual incapacity for accurate dereferencing. This is complicated by the fact that internalized reference-frames may guide too strictly in what one pays attention to and what one neglects. In such a state, the reference-frame controls the person and the person is not controlling the reference-frame. For me, the highest achievement in reference language usage is to recognize the full extent of my own possible dereferences in everything I say as I say it. This requires an attitude of interrogation and much practice. The idea is to keep a reference-frame in the status of tool. It is interrogation that allows me to 'cease to adhere' to a reference-frame so that I can control its use. I can then maintain it as a tool that I control, rather than sustain it as a framework that controls me. This is another way of saying that through interrogation I can learn the difference between what I know and do not know.

If I pose the question "Why does the book fall to the floor?" and the answer tendered is "gravity," no answer is received unless I can dereference 'gravity'. When I talk about 'gravity' the word is supposed to be a reference. 'Gravity' is like an address. We are like toddlers looking at a pointing finger, who are challenged to dereference the word 'gravity'. Other than associating this term with certain superficial sequence events, we find no dereference that derives from maturity of judgment within the context of experience. In other words, we do not know what 'gravity' is.

Data-Field. Dereferencing ultimately implies a data-field, the field of concern, the field from which we choose our matters-of-fact. What we pay attention to in the data-field I call matters-of-fact. It is our first phase of semantics. If we make a statement referencing matters-of-fact, the statement is the reference and the matter-of-fact is the dereference. If we also use matters-of-fact paradigmatically, then 'reference' and 'dereference' become immanently reversible in their possible applications. In other words, the *term 'tree'* may dereference to individual trees (schema or formula usage), or an *individual tree* may be used paradigmatically to dereference to other trees (paradigmatic usage). If we then assign a truth value to the statement, "Maple is a kind of tree," then it becomes a candidate for a premise in an argument.

How we may decide that a particular item of experience is a dereference is not easy to characterize but we generally include all possible differentiations as possible data. An actual datum is whatever we can pay attention to, it constitutes whatever we experience that we might be able to indicate (including concepts, imagination), it may be regarded as indivisible or as highly complex, as fuzzy or crisp. It is a candidate for making a statement concerning what we may pay attention to. Proceeding in this way we may discover foundation statements for new systems of thought, remaining vigilant for system generated artifacts.

What is Truth

In this context we may then ask, What is the dereference for truth with respect to systems of thought and their data-fields? Such a question revises the usual notion of Truth. Here we judge a truth relative to systems of thought. Here it takes on a definition that the naive question, What is Truth, does not suggest.

> **Note:** The question addressed in Plato's *Republic* is, "What is Justice?" A republic is constructed in order to have a context for defining the term 'Justice'. In an analogous way, systems of thought can be presented as contexts for defining the term 'Truth'.

Logic has a demarcation between the notions of validity and truth. It is possible that different systems of thought may spread over the 'same' data-field, or more precisely, two systems of thought may have the same data-field spread, though they have different modes of argument, different grammars, different modes of reference.

A mathematical example is given in the section on Experience Modifications (see above), where we may map every point on a plane with respect to a Cartesian frame of reference or with respect to a polar frame of reference. The definitions that distinguish these two reference-frames are based upon overtly agreed upon conventions. The formulas representing trajectories of a moving point for these two mapping systems are in different terms even when they are for the simplest representations, and furthermore, the respective formulas are incompatible. Even if we placed the zero points or any other points in coincidence, it may be true that these points relate to one point in the data-field, but the representation of the location is given by the reference-frames and the reference-frames are different. This does not mean that we cannot establish transforms between the two systems so that we can, in a manner of speaking, transform the representations in one system into corresponding representations in the other. This is a case where we conceive that the dereference is invariant but has a variety of possible reference modes.

That we can judge the reference modes as 'corresponding' suggests that the data-field has somehow been used as a reference-frame. The relation between the Centigrade (Celsius as revised by Linnaeus (Sweden) and Cristin (France), 1745) and the Fahrenheit temperature scales is a simpler example.

> **Note:** Celsius (Sweden) set $100°$ as the freezing point and $0°$ as the boiling point of water. A year later Linnaeus (Sweden) and Cristin (France) independently changed this around to $0°$ freezing and $100°$ boiling. Therefore, I argue this scale is better named 'Centigrade'. The SI committee did not know much science history in this case.

These scales exhibit two different quantitative conventions for the same data-field spread. In regard to representation there is no loss or gain in the accuracy of the representation between the two scales. There is just as accurate a representation in $212°$ F as in $100°$ C. To transform from one to the other scale is a simple formula; $F = (9/5)C + 32$ or $C = (5/9)(F - 32)$. This is also a case where the formulas work even if temperature is non-Eudoxian (non-linear)

But apodeictic systems also may differ in qualitative conventions. Different reference-frame modes differ in

their qualitative distinctions. Though we may find correspondences and modes of translating for qualitative differences, we find greater difficulty in translating between such
systems. Something may be lost, something may be gained.
And of course the worst scenario is to lose wanted representation and to gain unwanted representation. The Ein-
steins claimed that Newton's system is a special case of
Relativity, indicating that their theory of Relativity accounts for a larger scope of the data-field. Here the Ein-
steins claim a gain in wanted representation, a more com-
prehensive data-field spread.

One of the characteristics of the relation between the
Ptolemy system and the Copernicus system is that one is a
geometric transformation of the other. The two theories
have equal scope and equal difficulty. The losses and gains
in this transformation are discussed in detail in my *Star
Laws, Addenda: Duality Theory.*

With such a relativity of different systems for the
data-field spread, how can we speak of Truth which likewise must be considered in relation to different systems? At
least we should distinguish different truths relative to different systems of thought or show that there are no differences in this regard. If there are differences in mode of expression from system to system, or reference-frame to reference-frame, then truth, which we are accustomed to as-
signing to certain statements, is relegated to a relativity that
seems to subvert the possibility of dereferencing an 'invariant true statement.'

Invariant Truth. An invariant truth is one that is
independent of reference-frames or systems of thought. The
careful reader may say, Yes but what about the data-field?
Doesn't it remain invariant to changes made by reference-
frames? In coordinate geometry, in Euclidean space, and in
Newtonian mechanics we can, though not without some

difficulties, establish a theory of invariance. Within certain limits in a specific system of measurement, measuring the length of a finite straight edge yields the same number neighborhood no matter what Euclidean, Cartesian, or Newtonian reference-frame is used, as long as the unity is a common measure within the constraints of the specific system used. Or so it seems.

Data-Field Access. In a manner of speaking this length that is independent of other reference-frames and even independent of a unity as reference-frame, is a feature of the data-field. In a manner of speaking we could say that the data-field is invariant truth and is itself a kind of reference-frame. But this is only a manner of speaking because *when we consider the data-field we must also consider our access to it.* One limitation is already indicated by calling it a data-field. We presume a certain access to data. Data by its definition indicates anything that can be differentiated by us and represented either through concept or by image (concept and image are rigorously different as the concept of a circle and the image of a circle exemplify). Beyond this we cannot see.

Transcendental Knowing

In the past it has proven unwise to presume there is no beyond. This 'beyond' has been characterized in several different ways. One way is like the Kantian notion of noumena to which we can never have direct access. Another way is through instruments for mediate access data, data available to us only through instruments. For these arguments I shall ignore the Articles of Faith (a third notion of 'beyond').

We know there are data easily distinguishable with the unaided senses, but our powers of discrimination are limited. Our senses have limited ranges with different types of limitations for each sense, both qualitative and quantitative. For now it seems that these limitations are expressible in three dimensions; scope, resolution, intensity. All of these dimensions have size (ranges), size also admits non-linear scopes. Size is couched in time and space. Space, time, and contrast are conditions for measurement (Wittgenstein named 'color' as the third condition).

Some examples are given to clarify these terms.

Scope: With respect to seeing we have the spectrum of light; with respect to hearing we have the range of tones, etc..

Resolution: A synonym for resolving power, it is measured by the minimum difference at which a difference between two values is perceived, the difference between two colors (shade or hue), the difference between two sounds (timbre or tone), etc..

Intensity: With respect to seeing we have dimness and brightness; with respect to hearing we have softness and loudness (variations in amplitude), etc..

Size (*Scale, Range, Scope*): Scale is discussed below. Range states the quantitative limits for a quality. Scope is a set of qualities with their ranges.

Scale may impose a variety of constraints. Plotinus first pointed out largeness with respect to sound and Hemholtz was the first to measure it. With images at extremes we know for our senses some things are too dim or too bright, too small or too large, too close by or too far away, too fast or too slow for direct determination, etc. To view the Sun we use smoked glass, or indirect viewing, etc., to view dim stars we use time exposures or use computer enhanced images. Galileo showed that bigger may not be better, a larger lever may break under its own weight, he also showed how the shape proportions of bones require modification with size (scale), etc. Chemical engineers know that certain results obtained by mixing a few grams in laboratory conditions are not gotten when these same chemicals are mixed on an industrial scale. We can view plant growth through time-lapse photography, etc.

Transcendent Instruments. We develop instruments that we reason extend our perceptive powers in {scope, resolution, intensity} beyond the limitations of our natural senses. We now believe that our natural sense-ranges yield only a small fraction of the possible data-field. These instruments may bring us to new limits which we attempt to breach with even more refined instruments. In some cases some believe we have reached near ultimate limits that instruments will never have the occasion to measure beyond a calculated physical limit. Most physicists today believe that no material temperature is possible below a standard value for absolute zero. The Kelvin scale cannot have negative temperatures. No absorption or no dissipation of heat implies there is no transfer of heat or cold. To maintain 0 kelvins ('kelvin' is the unit, not 'degree') there can be no heat absorption and there is no heat to dissipate. These are supposed attributes of absolute zero.

It is difficult to eliminate the participation of the measuring apparatus in the creation of the 'observed' results, that is, the observer instruments influence the observed. A disregard of this possibility can lead to highly artificial theories. Microparticle physics suffers from this (I relate this in more detail in my *Star Laws, an Introduction to Convergence Buoyancy*). This disregard obfuscates the definition of 'empirical'. Galileo's telescope interpretations disrupted contemporary beliefs and his opponents argued that he could not prove his telescopes only magnified the target.

Independent Agreement. We like to suppose that investigators working independently of each other would come to the same determinations, a kind of invariance. Our satisfaction with regard to evidence and arguments presented in favor of this assertion depends much on a notion of standards that we have acquired in our experience. This includes standards in two modes, those relating to reference-frames for intelligibility (quality) and those relating to concomitant reference-frames for measurement (quantity).

Reference-frames used for measurement are known to be arbitrary within the latitudes of usability and are decided by convention. Reference-frames used for intelligibility are usually not thought of as so arbitrary because they form the very basis for how we see ourselves in our world; we live by them and through them. We do not want them to be arbitrary. It is reassuring when investigators working independently of each other can come to the same determinations. But is this illusion?

Modes of Control. In the trilogy of *knowing*, *doing*, and *understanding* we have three modes of possible control. What we know either controls us or we are in control of what we know. What we do is in control of us (therefore a happening) or we control what we do. What we understand happens to us or we can facilitate understanding (a form of control). This control is a matter of degree on a spectrum emphasis that varies from doings to happenings. If we can hold ourselves in the middle of this spectrum then we have a representation of doings-happenings where they have opposing force one on the other while we live in the hyphen. Living in the hyphen is a metaphor to recognize the two general forces that go into the mechanical aspects of our life as we live it. This hyphen is the position of Immanent Reversibility.

Modes of Thought: Reference-frames are instrumental for defining modes of intelligibility and they underpin our modes of thought. They are interfaces between the user and the data-field. There is no known limit to the number of possible designs for reference-frames for rendering an intelligibility to *unmodified experience*. The notions of truth, accuracy, and error are defined in terms of the reference-frame in use. These terms measure how well the particular reference-frame corresponds to the expectations it generates for the data-field.

Unmodified experience is functionally independent of any reference-frame. That is to say that there is no necessary relation between a reference-frame and the unmodified experience it interprets. There are many reference-frames that can be devised for determining an intelligibility for such experience. In other words, intelligibility is always in a state of relativity where its determinations depend on the architectonic of its reference-frames. Therefore truth, accuracy, and error are also relative to the reference-frame in use.

Knowledge and Truth

1. Reflecting on the presuppositions we make to determine that a test is acceptable or not for a given assertion, our first assumption is that assertions of knowledge must be testable.
2. Secondly, that this testing can only be used for showing that the assertion is disproved or not disproved.
3. This is to say that we cannot prove an assertion of knowledge; we can only show its robustness to critical arguments or critical experiments.
4. This test for robustness is far weaker than a claim for proof.
5. It implies that any assertion of knowledge remains in a permanent state of contingency and this includes any deductions made from the assertion.
6. A permanent state of contingency only allows us to say that so far the assertion has not been disproved.

7. This is the ultimate axiom of the Pragmatist.
8. If for modes of thought we divide the Universe into rationalists and empiricists we have two modes for Truth.
9. Truth for the rationalist is expressed in terms of necessary Truth.
10. Necessary Truth is determined by the formal methods of deductive Logic.
11. Truth for the rationalist is nothing more than an assertion of consistency in this Logic.
12. Rationalist Truth has its necessary connection within modified experience, and 'within' implies it is functionally independent of unmodified experience, i.e., there is no necessary connection with unmodified experience.
13. Truth for the empiricist is expressed in terms of contingent Truth.
14. Contingent Truth is determined by the robustness of an assertion to criticism (arguments or experiments), and is treated as truth as long as it survives criticism (based on unmodified experience).
15. Truth for the empiricist is the measure of effectiveness of an assertion as it applies to unmodified experience.
16. For consistency, the empiricist must treat modified experience as an artificial construct (a reference-frame).
17. These artificial constructs may be used instrumentally as long as they are found useful.
18. Modified experience expressed as a reference-frame can be used as an instrument for knowledge exploration, but it can also become an artificial barrier to other modalities of exploration.
19. If the empirical truth applies to a modified form of experience, the consistent empiricist confronts the modification with unmodified experience.
20. The effectiveness of the modification is either disconfirmed or not disconfirmed, but it is never proven.

END: *Lesson Three*

Pythagorean Silence
LESSON FOUR: Immanent Reversibility

OUTPUT, the problem of retrieval

1. Co-Extensive Exercise
2. Apodeictic Conventions
   a. Cultural Cloning
   b. Likely Stories
   c. Social Reference-Frame
3. Using Personal Interfaces
4. Immanent Reversibility
5. The Sentient Environment

LESSON FOUR: Immanent Reversibility

Introduction: The *Co-Extensive exercise* in this lesson is designed to intensify discriminatory skills. It is difficult but not impossible for beginners to practice this exercise without an experienced teacher or discussion group. The difficulty arises because of the necessity of judgment to discern the differences among **description, interpretation, evaluation**. This discernment is accelerated by having a discussion group or an experienced teacher who can help you see beyond the limits of your own judgment.

Co-Extensive Exercise

The Co-extensive Exercise is here defined as an exercise written, sketched, or oral in which you try to describe any given object in its descriptive detail and you reduce anything that smacks of interpretation or evaluation. In absolute terms, you cannot leave out shades of interpretation since all experience as understood by humans is based on interpretations of some sort. Likewise you cannot entirely rid yourself of evaluation since likes and dislikes have a strong influence on what we pay attention to and what we neglect. The goal is to attenuate or minimize these aspects that are interpretative or evaluative. Put in other words, you attempt to indicate an object in the most public language available to you.

For example, if you call an object a 'tree' you have offered an interpretation of sensory data. "Tree" is an interpretation. The descriptive terms for the "tree" should only include sensory data terms. Try drawing a tree without using any lines. An artist can do this. Because the drawing is not the tree, something by necessity is left out of the drawing. This emphasizes a limiting aspect for descriptions of any kind that are used for referencing an experience.

In regard to a tree, its colors (or shades of gray), shapes, aromas, sizes, etc., may be *descriptive*. To say it is a tree is *interpretive*. To say it is a beautiful tree is *evaluative*. We may evaluate descriptive aspects or interpretive aspects. In general, evaluations of experience are the easiest to remember (feelings enhance recollections), interpretations are second easiest (closure enhances recognitions and recalls), descriptive details are usually the most difficult to remember. Today you may remember that a book that you have read a number of years ago was a 'good book' yet you find it difficult to remember the details that led you to that conclusion.

Co-extension in memory has the sense of existing all at the same moment in time. In a sense, co-extensive memory is memory regarded independently of time. In this sense, all memory can be regarded as co-extensive before it is accessed and interpreted through time.

The Co-extensive Exercise adds precision to the Trobriand Exercise. These two exercises thus complement each other.

Description, Interpretation, Evaluation. In a verbal form the superficial dereference for this task is to write a *description* as free from *interpretation* and *evaluation* as you can. The evaluative terms such as 'beautiful', 'charming', etc., are easy to eliminate. In a manner of speaking you can kick them out the door, but on reflection you will discover that other modes of evaluation come in through the windows. Whenever we hold our regard on any scene, it is attracted to this and that sector in a manner that often suggests a spectrum of preferential treatment as we look at one part longer than another. This is a kind of hierarchal imposition that may be in part arbitrary and in part due to our natural sensitivities mingled with our learned habits. This imposition of a hierarchy supplies an infrastructure used for obtaining a perspective that opens the door to interpretation.

Without specifying the which is which source of preferences, we find ourselves in another spectrum that runs between nature and nurture, which is to say that these basal preferences in terms of degrees of attention and neglect are from a combination of born sensitivities and acquired habituations. This suggests the question of whether these preferences and imposed hierarchies can be flattened into a viewing without perspective. Thus the term 'flattened' perspective can be used for indicating no perspective. This would remove the underpinning requirements for interpretation. It is only through perspective that we have the foundation required for discerning movement, shapes, and shades of color. From these we interpret trees and frogs and etc. The blunt interpretations, thought to be straight forward, can be cast out.

When is description not interpretation?

As with evaluation perhaps the only thing we can hope for in this exercise is to attenuate interpretation. We can allow shades of colors and abstract shapes as the basal elements of interpretation useable for description. In this manner we can say what something looks like in terms of simple shapes and shades of color but we are not allowed to say what it is. Describing what something looks like must thus be done without any indication or hint as to what it is. Once we state what it is we are in the realm of interpretation proper. And once we use the common terms of evaluation we are directly asserting its affects on our emotions, a private experience that may or may not be shared with others and has the least probability of being common to all humans. Even interpretation can have individual variations among various people and there can be disagreement. However, language is based on the agreements that we have on interpreting something as an object and on the agreements about what that object is. Without a sufficient quantity of these agreements we would be hard-pressed for a language as well as hard-pressed for a culture and the art of translation from one language to another would have no foundation.

Here we may be struck by the notion that our general physiology has strong affects on our behavior and requires sufficient similarities among us to render translations possible. We find many differences in the social contract of marriage in various cultures, but even the differences in ceremony do not disallow a translation for the term 'marriage'. With the proliferation of television the variety of possible human actions is exploited in large degree and repetition of themes and events become evident to anyone with a memory. Originality is found but not so often. A set of characters play out the various possibilities of their assigned identities and often the program is then dropped for another set of characters to play out their possible variations of experience. In large part the teleplays display human life in its most cliché forms. If the audience had nothing to identify with they likely would have no interest in watching the program. Perhaps the most irritating tool in the situation comedies is canned laughter where laughter ensues at the slightest offhand remark, yet in a full room of watchers no watcher laughs. The laughter in these no-talent scripts has degenerated to being a part of the script.

This suggests that within a limited environment of family, friends, and places, that human activity has strong limits of possible expression. These limits may only be vaguely expressible but they can be seen in the majority of a population of people who seek security in the stability such limited environments offer. Usually such people have little use for newcomers or people of different habits, in fact these environmental restrictions introduce an extreme insularity held with pride and prejudice. In general, such mentalities are not good travelers.

For most verbal communications, interpreted objects function as a form of short-hand. We can use the term 'door' for some object and then add characteristics that augment its individuality. When people offer descriptions laced with interpretations we are left to construct a dereference for this description. For visual descriptions this dereference is essentially non-verbal and it has the possibility of being represented in quite different ways in spite of any textual bias.

Consider the following example. I am driving up a road and ahead I see a woman and two young children, a boy and a girl. The boy and girl appear to be attacking the woman. Though I might assert that the woman is the mother of these children, this supposition transcends the what-is-seeable. On passing nearer I hear the woman with raised voice saying, "Get that bee! Get that bee!"

Here I can infer that the children are quite obedient and attempting to help the woman. Though it raises the probability that the woman is their mother this inference remains contingent upon further evidence. She might be their nanny, etc. If I had a mind-set on the attack interpretation then the discovery that the children were helping her is rendered more astonishing by the reversal of terms from "attacking" to "helping."

When anyone offers a text based on visual description we generally picture some non-verbal representation of it. The best writers tend to be those that can elicit vivid non-verbal imagery from their verbal 'descriptions' of a visual experience. In effect, this takes us in full circle and we are back to the non-verbal imagery described in Lesson 1, but this time it is constructed rather from our history of dereferencing verbal representations of non-verbal direct experience. The constructed experience and the direct experience can both happen to us and often the things we deem known to us are a mixture of the two. It is also possible that constructed experience is something that we can do and in this case we are involved in the constructive use of imagination. However, these constructions vary across the spectrum of myth to science.

These statements do not preclude the function of closure in rendering our direct experience holistic and therefore coherent. There is less artifice in these closures that happen to us. Constructed experience on the other hand is full of artifice and in a sense introduces fictions into our catalog of claimed knowledge. We can cease to adhere to these constructions through interrogation. Learning to differentiate between constructed experience and direct experience is facilitated through interrogation. This is one of the most effective methods for yielding its presence. These constructions often function as our presuppositions that guide our thoughts. Language is a construction and it is one of the main theses of Benjamin Whorf and Edward Sapir that language influences the way we think. As we obtain more self-awareness it is we who turn this around and start to control our language. If we see a 'knife', what would allow us to see it as usable for a screwdriver?

Apodeictic Conventions

As noted before, we shall keep close to the original Greek, 'αποδειξις', 'a setting forth', 'arguments in proof of'. Thus conventions used for proof or for instructional exhibition are *apodeictic conventions*. Because they are conventions, their proper usage is mediate rather than direct. This is like using language as a pointing finger. First you see the pointing finger, then you look for the address pointed to, then you identify what you find there. These steps, no matter how quickly they are performed, render the convention mediate rather than direct.

Reference-frames for intelligibility that are couched in language are expressed with all the arbitrariness of language, of words, and of grammar. A language, a particular system of words and grammar, may influence the interpretation of any further experience, may order thoughts in ways that include systemic induced error, may impose a system generated bias. A word like 'sunset' may disposition us to regard the Sun as moving around the Earth rather than opening our thoughts to the dual possibility that the Earth rotates. When this occurs, it is not us who are in control of our language use; it is our language that is in 'control' of how we think (cf Friedrich Nietsche (1844-1900), Edward Sapir (1884-1939), Benjamin Whorf (1897-1941)).

Accepted social behavior deemed 'constructed', 'artificial', or 'formal', is a matter of convention. When through

practice we finally act in a seemingly natural and spontaneous fashion we say that these conventions have been 'internalized' and insofar as the structures are used automatically, through habituation or habits of expression, the degree of this internalization may be estimated. Automatism
in conventional usage indicates an interpretation through an
internalization of the convention when the automatism is a
matter of learned behavior of any kind. It is this internalization that renders us fluent, but it can also render invisible to
us the possible identifications. Habit makes efficient, but it
can also make blind. Furthermore, when you are used to an
environment you can become blind to certain things in it
from a kind of saturation. There may be an aroma for the
atmosphere, but we cannot detect it. It is an aroma lost to us
through a saturated experience.

A convention is an artificial device. Its artificiality
implies a kind of arbitrariness. This arbitrariness admits a
kind of fictional aspect; something invented or made up
(whether intentional or unintentional). When we become
aware of this invention aspect we find the possibility of a
kind of freedom from it. This freedom is a ceasing to adhere to the immediate dictates imposed on us by our learned
conventions, our heritage. We may abstract ourselves from
it and think about it. But habit can interfere with this 'ceasing to adhere'.

Cultural Cloning. *In communities where cultural
cloning is most successful we find the least changes in conduct.* In its extreme form cultural cloning is a form of death
to the evolution of a society. Without evolution such communities can only create an anthill.

> **Note:** The Harappan culture (Mohenjo-Daro, Harappa, etc.) seems to be
> one of these static ant-hill societies. In spite of the fact that they had run-
> ning water and sewage systems, they had no significant changes for the 500
> years that they thrived, and no sign of decor. Even their bricks remained

one-size never-changed oven-baked bricks. The few art objects found were
likely acquired through trade.

The obstacles to cultural cloning may be characterized as exterior and interior to the person. They range from
the teaching of liberal attitudes to the inadequate assimila-
tion of the culture one is born into, to acquaintance contact
with foreign cultures, to shocking experiences, to wars, or
natural disasters, etc.

Conventions, Visible and Invisible. Our conventions define our civilization. Most civilizations have forceful sanctions for individuals who do not respect the accredited conventions. It is through interrogation that we can put
conventions back into their proper place of mediate devices
for civilized life. This form of ceasing to adhere turns you
into an observer of your *internalized conventions*. We
might define the level of a civilization by the measure of
how explicitly its elders teach conventions as conventions.
A predominance of conventions invisible as such would
signal a lower civilization of mostly participants. A predominance of conventions visible as such would signal a
higher civilization with a greater number of observer-
participants. Unfortunately, this demarcation harshly places
every known civilization on the face of the Earth into the
lower category. An observer that interrogates conventions
can produce destabilizing effects not wanted by the general
public or the government of a given society.

Apodeictic conventions, as conventions, inherit a fictional aspect, a kind of freedom for invention. Apodeictic
conventions themselves may become restricting principles
in a certain mode of thinking, forming an adherence to a
way of reasoning that does not adhere to matters-of-fact.
This possible form of freedom with respect to science is pe-
jorative. This is why Aristotle believed that with knowledge (science) one loses freedom. If you 'know' the way

things are then you lose the freedom of choosing another way of knowing the way things are. The question is, can we know the way things are?

Likely Stories. The impetus to create likely stories has never been adequately explained. Ingenious minds early set themselves to inquire how experience is to be accounted for. Intellectual history is regarded by some scholars as a history of development from mythology to science.

Some ground of justification or explanation is thought of, i.e., a likely story that seems to account for an experience and seems to reconcile it with the current state of beliefs. Sometimes a description is given of an occurrence but its likely story, the story that accounts for it, changes. With time, different stories evolve that become more effective in their applications, displacing those with less power. Even with social resistance a kind of selection natural to social structures can occur here. Then the understanding adapts itself to the new story that has been found for explanation, and the description receives a new life and in time the description gets modified to fit the new story better.

This series of events is exemplified in the genesis of theories for celestial mechanics. For example, this kind of change in explanation is shown in part by Kepler's kinematics laws of planetary motion. Kepler's explanation was displaced by Newton's explanation. Another example, the Lorentz transformation; Lorentz's explanation was displaced by Einstein Relativity, etc.

Social Reference-Frame. We like to believe that in science our knowing moves toward invariance with respect to any particular social reference-frame. Just as logicians want to believe that a proposition or logic system is invariant to any particular language it is expressed in, scientists want to believe that a science law or science-system is invariant to any particular social reference-frame it is expressed in. Insofar as it is not, it is not science.

Thus we may say that scientific meaning or intelligibility for a science-system derives from its social reference-frame but it is always expressed in an apodeictic reference-frame that is intended to be independent of any particular society, we want this independence as well for our sensing of the data-field. If this independence is achieved then it would represent the demarcation between what is science and what are social beliefs. This is not concluded from a history of how science came into being but rather a stipulation that no scientist would want to deny.

Using Personal Interfaces

Most of us have a repertoire of interfaces that we use for communications. We usually interface with the boss in a manner different from the interface used with family members. We may even have a distinct interface for each person we relate to. If you overhear two friends talking about you as if you were two different people, either you have been using two distinct interfaces, or your friends each rendered a distinct interpretation from the same interface.

If we ever get into a social situation where we feel uncomfortable or awkward this feeling can often be attributed to requiring an interface that is not in our repertoire. It may seem that one could with continued exposure develop a new interface fitting the situation, but this may not be the case. There are many varieties of existence to be found in the mega-societies of today and with these varieties we find definatory prides and prejudices that can produce forceful modes of exclusion.

Your interface includes not only how you talk, but how you walk, your facial gestures, your hand gestures, your physical fitness, where you place yourself in the pecking order (with your mate, your children, your boss, your clients or students, your friends, etc.), your level of education, and may require consideration to your mode of dress. The scope you have with these features define the possibilities for the interfaces you can construct. The use of these features can be classed as automatic or intentional. These characteristics can be used for defining a repertoire of personality stereotypes. Here we consider five general types:

1. Alcibiades Type. An extreme case of versatility is when an individual identifies dynamically with whatever role is being played. Alcibiades is said to have lost himself through this form of identification. When in Athens he was Athenian, when in Sparta he was more Spartan than the Spartans, in Persia more Persian than the Persians, who was he? I call these personalities 'chameleons' and in its pathological interpretation the *Alcibiades Complex*.

2. Odysseus Type. People who, like Odysseus, have a plasticity that allows consciously choosing adaptations according to feed-back and feed-forward in order to facilitate situations actively without dimming the Seer that he is. Odysseus never loses awareness of his identity no matter what presentation he shows to others. In its pathological form this person is a permanent manipulator who never shows who (s)he really is. This I call the *Odysseus Complex*.

3. Achilles Type. Those who have no such plasticity fall under another difficult type who refuse to make adjustments to particular situations. Like cement they become set in their ways. In its pathological form I call it the *Achilles Complex*. Such inflexible individuals often have self-imposed tragic lives.

4. Socially Adept. Adept people are in some degree chameleons and in some degree they can be manipulative.

They may also hold aspects inflexible (such as their moral stance). Within these limits they adapt their personality according to the immediate contingencies perceived in their social universe, but not so far as to lose their sense of identity in their presentation. Their shifts tend to be shifts in emphasis. In its pathological form, habituation may render their existence mechanical and turn them into *sleepwalkers*.

5. Socially Inept. It is the immediate social situation that dictates the interface adjustments required for effective communication, but the inept lack the skills for such adjustments. This is different from people who simply refuse to adjust. *The socially inept, due to ignorance, lack the skills for reasonable interface adjustments to their social situation.*

These character types recall Shakespeare's notion that all the world is a stage. It helps understanding other people better if we spend some time acting in plays. It is a way of opening us to sense what it is like to stand in another person's place. This opens the way to an interrogation that can lead to ceasing adherence to your own character. This does not imply losing your character, but it does make you a better traveler.

Existential Conditions. When Aristotle discusses the concept of Being he teaches us that Being cannot be an attribute of an object since it is the condition for the existence of the object. A condition for the existence of an object cannot itself be an attribute of that object even though our habits of thought try to discuss the condition as if it were an attribute. Recursion is a self-reflexive state (calls back on itself). If we allowed the condition for the existence of attributes itself to be an attribute then this recursive call puts us into an infinite loop of ever previous conditions.

Kant, using the notions he learned from Swedenborg, uses space and time as conditions for human experience, in effect, conditions for human knowledge. Therefore, in his universe of discourse, space and time cannot be attributes of human experience since they are the conditions for that experience to exist. Wittgenstein adds 'color' as a third condition for human experience.

Conditions for the Sentient Environment.

Sentient Stance. In most religions 'faith' from its members is one of the binding requirements for obtaining the promises offered by the doctrine. Those initiated into membership may find that their entire life as members requires this faith. It never changes to knowing. For Pythagoreans this is not the case. Learning the Pythagorean doctrine is based on the acquirement of knowing, and knowing rids one from the state of faith. Faith for the Pythagorean is something to be rid of. You only accept as yours what you have found out for yourself. This is the *sentient stance*.

From within the Sentient Environment it seems that the individual soul and the Universal Soul are its conditions for existence, both co-extensively and synchronically (Spatial and Temporal states). From within the Sentient Environment we do not just feel their presence, they are the presence.

As conditions for the Sentient Environment they are not properly treated when treated as attributes (which renders them as objects), because conditions for objects cannot have that status. If we allow conditions for objects to be treated as objects we are caught in an *ad infinitum* recursion loop. It is the projection of language limitations that force us to speak of these states in a manner that resembles our references to objects. If we get too attached to these words we get stuck into one of the great limitations of natural language where every experience is expressed in terms of subject-object. Natural languages are not built for referencing the Universal Soul or the individual soul, which are the conditions for the Sentient Environment.

This does not preclude that from the manner of presenting the individual soul as couched in the Universal Soul we could mechanically conclude that the Universal Soul is the condition for the individual soul. The problem with this is that it requires backwards reasoning from our natural starting position. The natural starting position is the Sentient Environment, which is conditioned by both the individual soul and the Universal Soul. The Sentient Environment is not something we construct or invent. The Pythagorean exercises rather lead to a recollection or rediscovery of the way we are. My Sentient Environment is not the condition for my existence; my Sentient Environment is my existence.

Immanent Reversibility

This treatise maps a way to the Pythagorean Silence, the preparatory state for putting us in the position of our Sentient Environment. Once the Pythagorean Silence is obtained, positioning us in our Sentient Environment follows without desire or further effort. This is because the preparatory state, the Pythagorean Silence, removes the obstructions that blind us to our natural state. Once these obstructions are removed our vision opens to the Communion of our individual soul with the Universal Soul. Our awareness of this Communion no longer blocked, we find ourselves centered within it.

The practices described herein take on both aspects of our spiritual existence. On the one hand there is emphasis on the individual soul; on the other hand there is emphasis on the Universal Soul. What becomes one in their Communion can be treated aspectually as immanently reversible. This state of immanent reversibility allows us to recognize and intensify our own individual power and it allows us to intensify our affect on and use of the Universal Soul without adhering to either side of these aspects of our Sentient Environment. This is the state of the A and the not-A that is held functionally independent of contradiction through the state of immanent reversibility. Put simplistically, it is like opposite sides of the same coin.

Yoga is often misrepresented as doing away with the individual soul. It is true that those who identify with the Universal Soul can blind themselves to the individual soul. Those who identify with the individual soul can blind themselves to the Universal Soul. Most Indian pundits claim that the practice of Yoga leads to the disappearance of the individual soul because it is finally perceived as a delusion. For Pythagoreans all delusions and illusions are founded in the interpretations through the various possible *partitions of unmodified experience.*

In the Pythagorean Silence you are liberated from these partitions and all their associated interpretations. Then Communion ensues without further effort or desire. The state of Communion is your Sentient Environment.

The Sentient Environment

1. With Practice, the Pythagorean Silence can be generated by the self.
2. It is facilitated by the practice of a controlled form of sensory deprivation.

3. By closing off the distractions of the senses we are left with the Seer, which is apperception without sensory constraints.
4. This is our soul with no adherence to mind modifications.
5. This removes any of the access barriers to the Universal Soul.
6. Without desire or further effort this obtains Communion.
7. Communion is a state of immanent reversibility between the individual soul and the Universal Soul, which underpins our Sentient Environment.

The Exoteric and the Esoteric Schools

1. The Exoteric students study five years in preparation for the Esoteric School. These include the exercises in Lessons 1-4.
2. These studies include the Trivium and the Quadrivium and follow exercises for intensifying control for obtaining the Pythagorean Silence.
3. The Quadrivium includes geometry, astronomy, arithmetic, music; Astronomy is geometry in motion and Music is arithmetic in motion.
4. The Trivium includes logic, grammar, rhetoric.
5. After the completion of these five years of study the qualified neophyte is initiated into the Esoteric School.

END: *Lesson Four*

Pythagorean Silence
LESSON FIVE: The Yoga Sutras

LIBERATION: The Preparatory State for Communion

LESSON FIVE: The Yoga Sutras

Introduction. It is a mistaken belief among many yogis that the practice of Yoga somehow leads to the disappearance of the individual soul and that this somehow is a desired superior state. If this were the case then this practice would be nothing more than an unjustly glorified form of suicide. And because what actually occurs is quite out of our ordinary notions of experience our only recourse in trying to indicate the purpose of the Pythagorean Silence has to take the form of simile or metaphor.

The four written Sutra Books each end with a summary definition of the Pythagorean Silence. In effect, each one is from a different perspective. The first is *Definatory*, the second is *Procedural*, the third is *Conditional*, and the fourth is *Generative*. These four aspects of the Pythagorean Silence are preparatory to what comes next. In a sense, what comes next is the subject of a fifth book that can never be written.

This Pythagorean Silence is the quieting of all sensibility generated by the Attributes [Gunas] that provide the conditions to discern objects. These conditions are exterior to the Seer. The practice of this yoga takes the Seer to the state in which there is virtually no influence from these Attributes. This is a form of sensory deprivation. You lose sensing your body. In effect, your body becomes invisible to you (Sutra III:21). Your body is your sensory organ for your physical existence. With sensory deprivation you lose even the sensation that you have a body. This is what is meant by 'Discarnate' (Sutra I:19). The Attributes are so highly attenuated that, with concentration, the Modifications they generate can be ignored.

The Sutras do not continue beyond this Pythagorean Silence though this Silence is only a preparatory state. It is the preparation for recollecting Communion with the Universal Soul [Ishvara]. The supposition is that once this Liberation is achieved that the *recollection of Communion follows naturally without further striving or desire.*

Using a spatial simile, picture the individual soul and Universal Soul connected by a hyphen. The hyphen is the position of Communion. In effect, this Communion becomes recognized as the residence of the Seer. In it the Seer maintains its individual soul and the Universal Soul in a state of immanent reversibility (see Lesson 4). Thus this Communion becomes the *Sentient Environment.*

We can use another simile in an attempt to describe how the two are also one. In a holographic transparency we can represent three dimensional objects. If we cut the transparency into two pieces, each of the resulting pieces contains the complete image of the whole transparency. We can repeat this operation many times before the resolution of the image gets too dim to recognize. What we can conceive of for the Universal Soul that couches all individual souls is that the resolution does not diminish and that within each individual soul the entire image of the Universal Soul can be found. When it is found, the Sentient Environment is found in the Communion of the individual soul with the Universal Soul.

Note: Following the discipline of the Sutras for a number of years can obtain the Pythagorean Silence without the facilitation of a sensory deprivation experiment. Again a **warning**, if you attempt to facilitate the Pythagorean Silence through a sensory deprivation experiment and you have insufficient thought control training, the result can be a catastrophic disorientation.

In regard to the Communion state of the Seer, the sensing of individuality and the Universal Soul is a kind of co-extensive synchronicity that is a form of enhancement of the individuality and the non-individuality of the Soul. The Seer is I and not-I at the same time. This relation is like opposite sides to the same coin. Communion can be likened to a state of immanent reversibility where the Seer partakes of both the individual soul and the Universal Soul, and without contradiction. Those who Practice will know what I am saying.

Pythagoras founded retreats for facilitating Communion but these retreats were always temporary withdrawals from the noise of daily obligations. Here we emphasize that Pythagoras had no intention of teaching people to leave the World. The Communion, once achieved, is an empowerment that strengthens the Seer to influence and function within a World of sentient beings.

The Yoga Sutras form an outline for students who in ancient times memorized the Sutras and fleshed them out through discussion. These discussions were usually facilitated by a teacher who sparked the discussions with questions for students to consider. It was not for the teacher to impose doctrine. The students are left to discover within themselves the validity and worth of the doctrine. The Sutras become more and more intelligible to the student who practices in parallel the recommended regime for preparations (Lessons 1-4).

In comparing this rendition of the Sutras with others the student should note that all known commentaries are dated hundreds of years after the original text. Furthermore, commentaries are contrary to the original belief of the Pythagorean schools that use dialogue and a live discussion for bringing the text into the living context for a fuller understanding. Pythagoras did not want this doctrine to become a mechanical or ritualistic teaching.

One of the underlying purposes of this doctrine was to liberate sentient beings from a mechanical existence, from being virtual automatons, and awaken them to a capability for taking responsibility for their own lives. Rather than remaining mere creatures of internalized habits under the illusion that they are making choices when actually they are only fulfilling the shadows of childhood following the directions of ingrained habit, they progress toward taking the fullest responsibility available to them from the Sentient Environment.

Therefore, all such detailed commentaries (Sutra by Sutra) have been eliminated from this text. This allows the student understanding to evolve with Practice. The student is left to organize discussions that bring the doctrine to life.

The underpinning logic of the preparatory exercises is well known in schools that practice the Pythagorean doctrine.

Yoga Sutras of Patanjali (Pythagoras)
Note: For the following text, Seer = Soul; 'Mind' is a short form for 'sentient faculties'. Ultimate Seer, Universal Soul, and Ishvara (no gender) are synonyms.

BOOK I: On Control.

1. Now to explain Control [Yoga].

2. Control is a Ceasing to Adhere to Modifications of the mind.

3. Then the Seer stands within itself.

4. At other times the Seer identifies with the Modifications of the mind.

5. These Modifications are five; some are afflictions, the rest are not.

6. They are: Cognition, Illusion, Invention, Dormancy, and Recollection.

7. The elements of Cognition are: Discernment, Inference, and Testimony.

8. Illusion is mistaken cognition, knowing something as different from what it is.

9. Invention is carried on through words or thoughts and does not rest on an already existing instance.

10. Dormancy [Nidra] is when the supporting base for the mind is not present.
[**Translator Note:** The supporting base for the mind is conscious awareness. In effect Dormancy is a form of sleep-walking.]

11. Recollection is a reproduction of previous impressions without adding anything to them.

12. Control their influence by Practice and Cease Adherence to them.

13. Practice is the Exertion toward undisturbed calmness (absence of fluctuations).

14. With long constant persistence this Practice gains a firm foundation.

15. Ceasing Adherence [Vairagyam] to all objects seen or heard halts identification with them.

16. Perfecting these, the Seer [Perusha] Ceases Adherence to the Attributes [Gunas].
[**Translator Note:** The Attributes are required for sensing objects.]

17. Concentration to Comprehend a single Object [Samprajnata-Samadhi] requires Examination [Vitarka], Interpretation [Vicara], Gratification [Anandi], and the I-sense [Asmita].
[**Translator Note:** *Asmita* is the affirmation of Individuality *ex parte*, i.e., as separate from *Ishvara*]

18. The Practice of Stopping mental fluctuations renders a residue of attenuated Impressions [samskara].

19. In those who no longer sense their bodies (discarnates), it is in not-sensing the attenuated impressions that they are without objects.

20. With others [itaresam] this is preceded by faith [sraddha], vigor [virya], recollection [smrti], concentration (one-pointedness) [samadhi], and Comprehension [prajna].

21. Concentration and its results are most rapid to those who practice with intense commitment.

22. Even those with intense commitment have differences, since methods may be slow, or medium, or fast.

23. It also comes from intense devotion to the Ultimate Seer [Ishvara].

24. The Ultimate Seer is unaffected by affliction, action, accomplishment, or from attenuated impressions.

25. The seed of Omniscience is perfected in the Ultimate Seer.

26. The Ultimate Seer is the Teacher [Guru] of all teachers who have gone before, because the Ultimate Seer [Ishvara] is not conditioned by time.

27. The primal sound [pranavah] declares the Ultimate Seer.
[**Definition Note:** By tradition the primal sound is OM (or AUM). OM is not regarded as a word and therefore is never expressed as a word in the Sutras.]

28. While repeating this (sound), contemplate [bhavanam] what it declares.

29. From this comes the awakening of the individual soul (Seer) and the removal of barriers.

30. Sickness, incompetence, doubt, negligence, idleness, intemperance, erroneous discernment, inability to reach a stage of Control, or to hold it when reached; these mental projections are the barriers [antarayah].

31. Pain, despondency, body trembling, inhalation, exhalation, appear together with these projections.

32. To keep these back, practice on each of them.

33. For peace of Mind contemplate [bhavanatah] friendship toward the happy, compassion toward the sorrowful, goodwill toward the pure and be impassive toward the impure.

34. Or by exhaling and restraining the Breath [Prana].

35. Or with the emergence of a higher discernment of objects brings calm of Mind.

36. Or by a radiance from no adherence to sorrow.

37. Or by a Mind that does not adhere to its desires.

38. Or from underpinning knowledge from dreams [svapna] or dormancy [nidra].

39. Or by meditating on whatever thing one likes.

40. Mastery over this includes the smallest to the greatest.

41. Engrossment with respect to the discerner, the discerning, and the discerned, is like a gem that takes on the color of whatever it is near, and

this occurs when the fluctuations of Mind are weakened.
[**Definition Note:** Engrossment = absorbing one's attention].

42. When the mind mingles word [sabda], object [artha], and knowing [jnana], this is engrossment with exterior consideration [Savi-tarka].

43. When the mind dwells on an object [artha] from a pure memory, this is engrossment without exterior consideration [Nirvi-tarka].

44. By this the reflective engrossment [Savichara] and engrossment without words [Nirvichara], which have only attenuated objects, are also explained.

45. These attenuated Objects come to an end by non-manifestation.

46. These (four) are the only kinds of Engrossment concerning Objects.

47. On gaining proficiency in engrossment without words [Nirvichara], the inner instruments of discernment obtain clarity.

48. The Comprehension [prajna] gained in that state is fully factual [rtambhara].

49. This is different from the Understanding [prajnabhyam] obtained by Testimony or by Inference because it comes from instantiations.

50. The attenuated impression that generates from that obstructs other attenuated impressions.

51. Concentration without Objects [Nirvija-samadhi] avoids even this impression and this Ceases Adherence to all Modifications.

[**Translator's Note:** Sutra I:51 is a summary definition for the Pythagorean Silence. 'Nir-vija' literally translates to 'no-object'. Note that Book I is definatory rather than procedural and therefore does not instruct the student on how to proceed toward the Pythagorean Silence. The exigencies of how to proceed are given in Book II, the Book on Practice.]

BOOK II: On Practice.

1. Control in the form of action [Kriya-Yoga] includes Austerity [Tapas], self-examination, [Svadhyaya], and devotion [Pranidhanani] to the Ultimate Seer [Ishvara].

2. The aim is Concentration [Samadhi] to minimize the hindrances [Kleshah].

3. The five hindrances [Kleshah] are: misapprehension [Avidya], I-sense [Asmita], adherence [Raga], aversion [Dvesa], fear of death [Abhiniveshah].

4. Dormant, faded [tanu], suspended, or active, Misapprehension [Avidya] underpins the others that follow.

5. Misapprehension [Avidya] regards the transient as everlasting, the impure as pure, pain as pleasure, and the non-self as self [Atma].

6. I-sense [Asmita] identifies the powers of the Seer with the Mind as the same [ita].

7. Adherence [Ragah] results from pleasure.

8. Aversion [Dvesah] results from misery.

9. Innate even in the wise, Fear of Death [Abhiniveshah] is found alike in all.

10. Ceasing Adherence to these Attenuations [Suksmah] is through cessation of their mental production [Pratiprasava].

11. The cessation of these modifications [Vrittayah] is through meditation [Dhyana].

12. The underlying Karma impressions [Karma-ashayah] that are rooted in the hindrances grow into action in this life or in a life to be.
[**Definition Note:** Karma is the sum total of one's actions in life, said to be a determinant in one's destiny. It is now a global word found in many languages, including English.]

13. Birth, life-span, and experience is the result of that (Karma) remaining at the root.

14. Due to reverent and irreverent actions, this (Karma) can yield pleasure or misery.

15. To the discerning, everything brings misery either as a consequence of or in anticipation of lost happiness, or fresh yearnings from impressions of happiness; and also from opposition of Attribute [Guna] modifications.

16. Avoid Adhering to misery that has not yet come.

17. The Merging [Samyogah] of the Seer with things seen causes what is to be avoided.

18. Sensed Objects [drsyam] are for Experience [bhoga] and for Liberation [apavarga], and include the sense-faculties with their actions, and are diverse in Discernability [prakasa], Action [kriya], and Stability [sthiti].

19. The changing states [parvani] for the Attributes are various [vishesa] or not-various [avishesa], denoted [lingamatra] or not-denoted [alingani].

20. The Seer, when pure, sees only as a Witness, the modifications of the mind.

21. The nature of the discernible actually is that objects are for the Seer.

22. Though they are invisible to those who reach the goal, the objects are not gone since they are not invisible for others.

23. Merging [samyogah] the powers [sakyoh] of the owner [svami] and the owned [sva] brings awareness of its owned form [svarupa].
[**Translator's Note:** In the compound word *sva-svami-sakyoh*, *sakyoh* is in the dual form, which indicates that in this context *sva* and *svami* are treated as separate though juxtaposed concepts. *Svami* can also denote *Master*. From context; the self as 'owner' is the Seer, the self as 'owned' is the seen. *Rupa* is 'form' and 'form' derives from modifications.]

24. Ignorance is the cause of this (merging).

25. Liberation disengages the Seer from that (ignorance), and with that (ignorance) absent the merging is absent.

26. The way to Liberation is through an unwavering [aviplava] practice of discriminative discernment.

27. The ultimate [prantabhumih] comprehension [prajna] for that is sevenfold.
[**Translator Note:** The first seven branches of Control (Yoga).]

28. Eliminating impurity through Practicing the Branches of Control [yoga] brings the Light of Knowledge   [jnana]   to   discriminative discernment.

29. The eight Branches are: Restraints [Yamas], Observances [Niyama], Posture [Asana], Breath Suspension [Pranayama], Disengaged Senses [Pratyahara], Attention [Dharana], Meditation [Dhyana], Concentration [Samadhi].

30. The (Five) Restraints are these: no injury [Ahimsa], no lies [Satya], no stealing [Asteya], no intemperance [Brahmacharya], no possess-iveness [Aparigraha].

31. As major vows [mahavratam] these are universal and unrestricted by class [jati], place [desa], time [kala], or duty [samaya].

32. The (five) Observances are these: purity [sauca], serenity [santosa], austerity [tapas], self-examination [svadhyaya], and devotion [pranid-hanani] to the Ultimate Seer [Ishvara].

33. To counter inimical thoughts (to the Restraints and Observances) think on opposites [pratipaksa].

34. Injury, lies, theft, intemperance, envy; whether committed, caused, or approved through greed, anger, or ignorance; whether slight, middling, or great, cause unending misery and ignorance; they end [iti] with opposite [pratipaksa] thought [bhavanam].

35. All hostility ceases in the presence of one with the no-injury Restraint perfected.

36. All words gain the power of obtaining results for one with the no-lies Restraint perfected.

37. All treasures stand ready to serve one with the no-stealing Restraint perfected.

38. Energy [Virya] acquires to one with the no-intemperance Restraint perfected.

39. Awakening insight into the what and the how of   existence comes to one with the no-possessiveness Restraint perfected.

40. Practice of purification disengages one from bodily life and this disengages one from infatuation with the bodily life of others.

41. And this acquires Purity of disposition, Gratification for the mind, one-pointedness, disengaged senses, and fitness for self-awareness.

42. Fulfillment in this brings unsurpassed happiness.

43. By way of austerities, the Powers [Siddhih] of the body and senses come through the attrition of impurities [asuddhi].

44. Through repetition of self-examination [svadhyayat], the devotee bonds with the Divine within [Ista-Devata].

45. Concentration is perfected through devotion to the Ultimate Seer [Ishvara].

46. Posture [Asana] must be firm and agreeable.

47. With unlimited engrossment in tension free effort.

48. From that the obstruction from dualities [Dvandva] stops.
[**Definition:** Dvandvas: good/bad; beautiful/ugly; pleasure/pain; doings/happenings, etc.]

49. Once done, follow this with suspensions of the incoming and outgoing breath.

50. The exhalation and inhalation suspensions [stambha] and movements [vrtti], when observed [paridrstah] by location, duration, and number become extended [dirgha] and attenuated [suksmah].

51. This leads to a fourth that goes outside the realm of inhalation-exhalation.
[**Translator Note:** 49, 50, 51 concern breath regulation [Prana-yama]. Exhalation, inhalation, suspension are the first three.]

52. From that the veil over enlightenment attenuates.

53. Then the mind is fit to hold attention [Dha-rana].

54. Similar to the mind's owned-form [svarupa] separated into itself and its objects, the senses are disengaged.

55. Then mastery over the senses is complete.

[**Translator's Note:** Sutra II:55 is a summary for the procedural tool used for acquiring the state of the Pythagorean Silence. Note that Sutra II:54 recapitulates the procedural terms for the Pythagorean Silence. Note also that the conditions that derive from the Powers manifested through Practice are not discussed until Book III.]

BOOK III: On Powers.

1. Attention [Dharana] is holding the mind to a certain region.

2. Meditation [Dhyana] is a prolonged holding of the mind in that region.

3. Concentration [Samadhi] is when Meditation illuminates the essence of the object.

4. Perfect Meditation [Sanyama] is when these three, Attention, Meditation, Concentration, are exercised at once.

5. Comprehension [Prajna] comes from mastering this (Sanyama).

6. This power is distributed in ascending stages.

7. These three (Attention, Meditation, Concentration) are more internal practices than those previously described.
[**Previously listed I:29 and described first five Yoga branches:** yama, niyama, pratyahara, pranayama, asana].

8. But they are still exterior to Concentration with no Objects [Nirvijasya].

9. Thus with the mind arrested, the attenuated impressions are no longer visible to the Seer, and since these attenuated impressions remain active though unseen, the mind continues changing during that arrested state.

10. This continued changing caused by attenuated impressions thus assures that the arrested mind continues its existence though in an arrested state.

11. Diminish fluttering from one object to another and augment one-pointedness; this brings Concentration while the mind continues changing during its arrested state.

12. There again, since the past and the present Modifications are similar, the changing Mind has stability.

13. These explain the three changes in form, time, and state.

14. The past, present, and future form a medium for the changing Attributes.

15. Change of sequence causes differences in change.

16. Perfect Meditation on the three changes brings the knowledge of past and future.

17. When the word, its object, its concept, are all blurred together, applying Perfect Meditation on each as distinct obtains an understanding of the sounds uttered by all beings.

18. Perfect Meditation on your attenuated impressions obtains memory of previous lives.

19. Perfect Meditation on your impressions of another person gains knowledge of their thoughts.

20. But the basis for the thoughts do not get known because that is not the observed object.

21. Perfect Meditation on your body form inhibits seeing it, thus it renders the body invisible (to you).

22. The force generated by one's actions [Karma] may be delayed or operative immediately; Perfect Meditation on this reveals portents [Arishta] that warn you of possible harm or death.

23. Perfect Meditation on friendliness, and so on [adishu] (i.e., compassion, goodwill, and being impassive to the irreverent (I:33)) acquires strength.

24. Perfect Meditation on physical strength can bring the strength of an elephant, etc.

25. Perfect Meditation on radiant discernment (I:36) brings knowledge of attenuated objects, or things with obstructed view, or at great distance.

26. Perfect Meditation on the sun brings a knowledge of the Cosmos.

27. On the moon acquires a knowledge of the star patterns.

28. On the fixed pole-star acquires a knowledge of the motions of the stars.

29. On the navel plexus brings knowledge of the body composition.

30. On the trachea subdues hunger and thirst.

31. On the bronchial tube acquires stability [sthairyam].

32. On the light in the head acquires the vision of spiritual beings [Siddhas].

33. Everything becomes known from Intuition [Pratibhad].

34. Perfect Meditation on the heart acquires knowledge of the Mind.

35. Experience does not distinguish between the Mind and the Soul, but experience exists for the Soul; therefore, Perfect Meditation on the Soul acquires knowledge of the Soul.

36. This brings intuitive-discernment [pratibha] from the supernormal senses of hearing [Sravana], touch [Vedana], sight [Adarsha], taste [Asvada], smell [Varta].

37. The mind in its usual fluctuating state acquires these powers, but these powers impede Concentration [Samadhi].

38. Weakening the binding restraints of the mind and knowing the channels for mind activity, one can move the mind into another body.

39. Mastery of the life-force with upward direction [Udana] permits movement as without barriers in water or mud or thorns or etc., and assures that one can exit the body at will [utkrantih].

40. Mastery of the life-force that evenly distributes food in the body [Samana] can generate body radiance.

41. Perfect Meditation [Sanyama] on hearing and its medium [Akasha], obtains supernormal hearing.
[Definition Note: Akasha = substratum (medium)]

42. Perfect Meditation on the body, its medium [Akasha], and on becoming as light as cotton wool, one can traverse the skies.

43. Perfect Meditation on discarnate fixity [Mahavideha] removes the veil that conceals illumination from the mind.
[Definition Note: Mahavideha, in English 'discarnate fixity', is when the mind disengages from the body and is held functionally independent of the body (since your body is rendered invisible to your mind).]

44. Mastery over the elements [Bhutas] is obtained through Perfect Meditation on the gross properties, the fine properties, the holistic nature, the inherence of the Attributes, the Object contribution to the Soul's experience.

45. From that comes the power of minimization [Anima], etc., and from that the perfection of the body, and non-obstruction to Cosmic Order [Dharma].
[Definition Notes: Anima is here applied to an induced sensory deprivation, i.e., a minimization of sensory input. Dharma is the natural and moral order that applies to all beings and things. Pythagoras used the term 'Cosmos' for this universal order.]

46. Perfection of the body is in beauty, elegance, strength, and a rigid hardness.

47. Mastery over the Senses is gained through Perfect Meditation [Sanyama] on their Receptivity [grahana], their owned-form [svarupa], I-Sense [Asmita], Mutuality [Anvaya], Objectiveness [Arthavattva].

48. And from this a Mastery [jayah] over their original source [Pradhana] makes the senses function independent of the body, quickening the mind.

49. Perfect Meditation on the discernment between Mind [Sattva] and Soul [Purusha], comes all power over and all knowledge of (one's) being.

50. Ceasing Adherence even to this brings the seeds of misery to a standstill, which brings Liberation.

51. Lest you obtain undesirable consequences, reject from 'people of high position' [sthani] the invitations that inspire in you an attachment to your pride [smaya].

52. Perfect Meditation [Sanyama] on the moment and its sequence (precession and succession) brings discernment.

53. Two things not distinguishable because they look alike can be distinguished by difference in time and position.

54. Internalized Discernment [Taraka] has no sequence and encompasses all things from all times.

55. Equal Purity of Mind [Sattva] and of Soul [Purusha] end [iti] in Liberation.

[**Translator's Note:** Sutra III:55 is a summary definition in conditional terms of the Pythagorean Silence. How the Powers aid the generation of the Pythagorean Silence is given in Book IV.]

BOOK IV: On Liberation [Kaivalya].
Note: 'Mind' is used as a short form for 'sentient faculties'.
[Gunas: sattva, rajas, tamas] Gunas are the three primary Attributes of the Phenomenal World. Sattva = knowing; Rajas = changing; Tamas = holding.

1. Powers [Siddhi] are inborn, or made manifest through herbs, or incantations [mantra], or austerities, or Concentration.

2. The flowing in of natural powers is the transformation inherent at birth.

3. There is no cause for the flow of natural powers, but one can cause the removal of obstacles to the flow, as a farmer can cause the removal of obstacles to running water, which then can run by its own nature.

4. The created minds (in a person) generate from the pure I-sense [Asmita].
[**Translator Note:** Asmita is the affirmation of Individuality ex parte, i.e., viewed apart from Ishvara. These created minds relate to our repertoire of interfaces.]

5. Though various in their activities, the one original mind directs these different created minds.

6. Of these, those born of Meditation are free from any afflictive adherence.

7. Control [Yoga] actions are neither black nor white; other actions are threefold: black or white, or a mingling of these.

8. For the actions that are threefold the only feelings [Vasana] that can manifest are those that fit that action only.
[**Definition Note:** Vasana = impressions from feelings, i.e., what we sense from feelings.]

9. The correspondence between memory and attenuated impressions brings together actions that were separated by difference in nature, place, and time.

10. The desire for well-being is not conditioned by time and therefore has no beginning, therefore the feelings from which it arises have no beginning.

11. Held together by cause, effect, support, and objects, the feelings disappear when these are absent.

12. The fundamental forms of past and future are in the present and the only differences are in their forms taken at different times.

13. These forms are there at every moment and are composed of the three Attributes [Gunas], whether manifest or not noticeable.

14. From the coordinated changes in the three Attributes, an object appears as a unit.

15. The paths of material things and of states of consciousness are distinct, as shown from the fact that the same object may produce different impressions in different Minds.

16. Nor do material objects depend upon a single Mind, for how could they remain objects to others, if that Mind ceased to think of them?

17. An object is discerned, or not discerned, according as the Mind is, or is not, tinged with the color of the object.

18. Because the Soul does not change and is master of them, the modifications of the Mind are always knowable [jnatah].

19. The Mind is not self-luminous, since it can be discerned as an object.
[**Definition Note:** drsyatvat = discerned as an object]

20. Nor could the Mind at the same time know itself and things external to it.

21. If the Mind were illuminated by a more inward mind there would be an endless series of discerning minds, and a mix-up of their memories.

22. When the Mind mirrors the Seer it becomes conscious of its own intelligence.

23. The Mind understands every object when it mirrors both the Seer and the Seen.

24. From the many impressions understood in this combination the Mind no longer exists for itself.

25. Thinking of the Mind as Self stops when one knows this difference.

26. Then the mind inclines toward an awareness directed toward Liberation.

27. Breaches in this inclination let in other mind fluctuations due to attenuated impressions.

28. Remove these fluctuations the same way as taught for removing the hindrances.

29. With uninterrupted self-awareness one has no interest even in all-knowing and this brings the concentration [Samadhi] known as the Cloud of Cosmic Order [Dharmamegha].

30. From this (Cloud of Cosmic Order), all hindrances and actions [Karma] stop.

31. Knowledge freed from impurities unveils without limit and leaves little left to be known.

32. Attaining their purpose, the sequence of Attribute changes comes to a stop.

33. Sequence correlates to the moments and is discernable when these changes stop.

34. Deprived of purpose for the Soul, the Attributes return to their source; this instates Liberation in its owned form and this end [iti] brings Pure Awareness [citi-saktir].

[**Translator's Note:** 'Liberation' and 'Pythagorean Silence' are synonyms. Sutra IV:34 states the summary definition of the Pythagorean Silence in generative terms that requires the other three. *Citisaktir* suggests the recollection of Communion: *citi* carries the sense of pure awareness; *saktir* carries the sense of creates or brings to action.]

END: *The Yoga Sutras*

Epilogue

Learning Sanskrit. Note that though Sanskrit texts in Western schools use the Hindi script, we know that this was not the original Sanskrit script. By a tradition of uncertain length the original name of the Sanskrit script is 'Devanagari'. Kale (1894) suggested that the Devanagari was used for the Ashoka edicts, but this suggestion was made in ignorance of the fact that the edicts use a number of languages each in their own script. In the edicts, only the Greek and Aramaic scripts antedate the Mauryan Dynasty founded in late 4th Century B.C. There is no evidence that the other scripts existed before the Mauryan Dynasty was founded.

For the most part we have no direct access to most of these old language forms because our examples of them are sparse. This lack of examples renders translations a matter of guesswork based on similarities to known languages.

The Sanskrit pundits who teach us that the letters have no names do not seem to recognize that syllabary scripts do not need special names different from the syllable they represent. That the Hindi script is also called Devanagari does not imply that it was the original script.

The Hindi script would be better named 'Nagari' as Whitney suggests. Today, Sanskrit in India is written in whatever script is used in the region of study. Thus in West Bengal the Sanskrit texts use the Bengali script. In sum, the earliest syllabary fell out of tradition and therefore today it is no longer regarded as important which script we use. Even the English alphabet may be used. Cuneiform never reached India and it is a cuneiform syllabary that was used for ancient Persian. Since tradition lost the use of the first Indian Sanskrit syllabary the use by Europeans of the Hindi 'Devanagari' can be seen as another pundit misrepresentation of Sanskrit. Now only the Panini Indian Sanskrit grammar is used and the scripts are usually chosen from any of the current Indian scripts.

Sanskrit Grammars. The following list of Sanskrit grammars is just a starter list:

Sanskrit Grammar (1924), W. D. Whitney. He says of the Classical language (Paninized forms), "Of linguistic history there is next to nothing in it all; but only a history of style, and this for the most part showing a gradual depravation, an increase in artificiality and an intensification of certain more undesirable features of the language--such as the use of passive constructions and of participles instead of verbs, and the substitution of compounds for sentences." Whitney also complained that the followers of Panini were teaching the language backwards. One should not start with a grammar to generate sentences, one should start with natural sentences and generate a grammar. In this sense Whitney's Sanskrit grammar was a revolution in its approach to teaching Sanskrit. His Sanskrit grammar has a wide scope put into one succinct volume.

Sanskrit, A Teach Yourself Book (1973), by Michael Coulson who was a Sanskrit scholar at Edinburgh University. He purports to like the Panini grammar, "Acceptance of Panini's rules implied the final stabilization of the phonology of Sanskrit...and also of its morphology..." and he regards W. D. Whitney as, "...a great but startlingly arrogant American Sanskritist of the nineteenth century,..." Even so, Coulson copies Whitney's strategy of teaching from sentences to the grammar rather than the Panini generative style of going from grammar to the sentences. Coulson's examples only come from Sanskrit plays, which makes his scope narrower and easier than Whitney's. The peculiarity of Sanskrit in plays is that the elite speak in Sanskrit but the commoners speak in Pakrit.

A Higher Sanskrit Grammar (1894) by Moreshwar Ramchandra Kale, is a good introduction to a university standard grammar and he praises the grammar of Panini. The text is in English but the student is expected to have prior knowledge of so-called Devanagari, the Hindi letters he uses for writing Sanskrit. This in part confirms that the book is written for Hindu students. He freely copies and modifies the work of other grammarians, both Western and Indian, to fit into his course presentation, but he acknowledges this use. It also tells us that he is eclectic in his presentation.

Sanskrit, Essentials of Grammar and Language (1934), by Kurt F. Leidecker, M.A., Ph.D. Anchorite Press. This is the most succinct overview of the Sanskrit language ever published in book form. For the student impatient to get into the language, it presents a quick overview and fairly good groundwork for further study.

Sanskrit Dictionary

A Sanskrit-English Dictionary, Sir Monier Monier Williams (1894). Motilal Banarsidass. Composed by one of the great Sanskrit scholars of the 19th Century, this remains the most complete Sanskrit-English dictionary still in print.

Patanjali in English for Comparison

Because the *Yoga Sutras* are preserved in Classical Sanskrit, an ancient foreign language, readers who want to read Patanjali in English are faced with difficulties in choosing the best rendition. The availability of an accurate English translation of Patanjali's *Yoga Sutras* is hard to find. There are two general categories for renditions, those who have made a study of Sanskrit and those who have not.

The following pioneer English translations from the Sanskrit can be used for comparisons:

Woods, *The Yoga-System of Patanjali*,
Rama Prasada, *Patanjali's Yoga Sutras*.

On the Dire State of English Translations of Patanjali

Worst Western Editions. Among Western editions there is a proliferation of renditions made by people who know little or no Sanskrit. The least useful American rendition is by Archie Bahm who seems to know little Sanskrit and in my opinion shows no holistic understanding of what these Sutras are about. He has a PhD in Philosophy. He is inconsistent in his use of technical terms of Yoga (Control) and for many of the Sutras he has invented an interpretative rendition and re-organization that loses much of the sense of the original Sanskrit. Therefore his book with his commentaries is not very useful for serious study.

There is an Irishman, Charles Johnston, who uses terms that for me show a degree of illiteracy, or an exaggerated poetic license, such as 'vesture' (he does not seem to know this word is a reference to clothing) and 'poise' where the word should be closer to some notion of 'body posture'. He claims some knowledge of Sanskrit, but this is not so evident in his rendition. He invents a number of his own term correspondences, which often only have a vague correspondence to the Sanskrit. For me this adds obfuscation to the underpinning logic of the text by someone who sometimes gets the gist of it and other times does not. His rendition is available free on-line.

Indian Editions. Among the Indian pundits there is a lack of skill in rendering the text into English as shown by keeping the Sanskrit technical terms with no English rendering for them in their so-called translations of the Sutras. Furthermore, there is a tendency among them to use stilted English with many extra words. One line of Sanskrit can turn into six lines of English. Because they often cannot find the proper English phrase they appeal to many insertions under the claim that they are keeping close to the Sanskrit meaning. Their commentaries tend to be biased toward their own favorite forms of Yoga. Furthermore, their commentaries tend to be very wordy and often obfuscate rather than clarify the Sutra. This suggests that the pithy Sanskrit text evades their understanding. It is true that an occasional insertion can help intelligibility, but their usage of insertion is so frequent that again it seems indicative that they could not find an appropriate English phrasing.

Swami Vivekananda published a book under his name called *Raja-Yoga*, in which he purports to present the Patanjali text in English. Most of the current translations use an edition where the Book III lists 55 Sutras and Book IV lists 34 Sutras. In the third book Vivekananda lists 56

Sutras and in the fourth book of the Sutras he has only 33. No, the odd Sutra out was not put in Book III. Though it is possible that he wrote the comments, it is doubtful to me that he was the translator of the text. In many places the translation is a rather weak rendition that barely corresponds to the Sanskrit. There is no indication in his biography that he ever studied Sanskrit to the degree required for translating Patanjali. The Theosophists seem to have used his numbering of the Sutras. Even so, he was successful in gathering millions of dollars for his 'Vedantist' sectarian Yoga for which he built a temple in San Francisco. He led the way for other 'pundits' to make millions in America, such as Sri Aurobindo, Krishnamurti, Maharishi, etc.

Swami Hariharananda Aranya is a higher class pundit who provides a commentary on these Sutras. He wrote in Bengali. His book is organized with a glossary in a way that allows the student to follow the technical Sanskrit terms. His translator to English, P. N. Mukerji, kept the Sanskrit terms that the Swami kept, which gives the English rendering a semi-English presentation. In the English parts we again find stilted phrasing and many extra words that show the attempts of the translator to maintain the phrasing of the original Bengali edition. The final English form can be rough going for the beginner. It is a worthwhile book for study as it offers an acquaintance with the many important technical terms found in the original Sanskrit. Furthermore, there is an effort to keep the interpretation close to the Sanskrit, even maintaining some of the structural obfuscations introduced by the Panini grammar. One of the Swami's biases is Hatha Yoga, which his commentary details to exaggeration when Patanjali speaks of posture.

Note: Probably the best posture is just lying on your back in a comfortable bed. The idea is to find a relaxed position that does not distract from rendering the disappearance of the sensing of your body, which is your physical sensory apparatus. This is what is meant by 'Discarnate'. In effect, your body becomes invisible to you.

Comparison of English Renditions for Sutra I:51

Archie Bahm I:51
"Sutra LI
(Finally), when even the enjoyment by the mind of the Truth itself is given up, then one's consciousness is utterly without seed."

Johnston I:51
"51. When this impression ceases, then, since all impressions have been ceased, there arises pure spiritual consciousness, with no seed of separateness left."

Vivekananda I:51
"51. By the restraint of even this (impression, which obstructs all other impressions), all being restrained, comes the 'seedless' Samadhi."

Swami Hariharananda Aranya I:51
"By The Stoppage Of That Too (On Account Of The Elimination Of The Latent Impressions Of Samprajnana) Objective Concentration Takes Place Through Suppression of All Modifications. 51."

Ross Lee Graham I:51
"51. Concentration without Objects [Nirvija-Samadhi] avoids even this impression and this Ceases Adherence to all Modifications."

The Status of Indian Scholarship

The Hindu religion emphasizes escaping from the Wheel of Life, while most Western minds would praise the Wheel of Life and would welcome reincarnation if they found it available. It should not be surprising that a culture that emphasizes escape from the Wheel of Life should have no interest in history. It is doubtful that a culture that has so little interest in history would be bothered with writing epic poems, mythic or not, since epics have the form of a narrative history.

The most severe criticism of Indian scholars, and notably of the Brahmin scholars, is found in Hegel's *The Philosophy of History*, where he reports the manufacture of false Sanskrit documents for selling to Western researchers, a dishonesty in wide practice in the 19th Century. In his severe accusations he states that the typical Indian scholars are liars and cheaters and he follows this with what he regards as hard evidence for these accusations. Though we would like a tamer view of this surreptitious activity we cannot escape the fact that for the better part of two Centuries many Western scholars have been duped by misrepresentations.

Young scholars, who lack the knowledge and patience to check for source credibility, are still following secondary sources of native writers who make claims that go beyond any available evidence.

We have an important obstacle to obtaining an accurate Indian history that starts with the mythological history created by the Brahmins over the many years of English dominion over them. These Brahmins pretend that this nonsense history (revealed by foreign sources and archaeology as fabrications), represents a documented history. They pretend that their culture (culture of the Brahmin), which had never before shown any respect or interest in history, actually had a history documented by native scholars.

The problem of 'history' for these pundits was put before them from Western scholars who asked questions about their history for which they had no answers. They were offered money for answers so they started inventing answers. Their fabrications even get support from young Western scholars who are unaware of this long history of dishonesty. In effect, these young Western scholars help promulgate nonsense by depending on the testimony of the Indian scholars who support these misrepresentations.

One of the errors generated by misrepresentation of Indian history concerns the alleged entry of Aryans into the Ganges valley stretching between Pakistan to the West and Bangladesh to the East. All three of these territories allege the important presence of Aryan descendents. Today it is declared in their pseudo-histories that the Aryans invaded India around 1500 B.C. Furthermore, prior to archaeological counter evidence the pundits claimed an even more ancient Aryan invasion.

It is here we shall follow Hegel's advice, that if we want to know any truth concerning Indian history we must first begin with the foreign sources and ignore the native sources that do not correspond to more reliable testimony. We also demand correspondence to archaeological excavations.

Concerning the alleged invasions of Aryans in northern India we look back to Alexander the Great. Arrian reports in his *The Campaigns of Alexander* that when Alexander came in contact with the Indians that "...they are darker-skinned than any other race except the Ethiopians, and the finest fighters to be found in Asia at that time." This leaves us to wonder when the so-called Aryan invasions occurred. Surely these darker-skinned Indians cannot be Aryan stock.

Furthermore, the Brahmin that Alexander encountered were not light-skinned either. They were as dark as all the other Indians. Nor were they identified by caste as the caste system did not yet exist. They were recognized as Brahmin by their function as priests or as the Greeks called them, philosophers. In spite of their illiteracy, Alexander the Great respected them and regarded them as wise men. They were not distinguished by the color of their skin. The conclusion is that if there were Aryan invasions *the first Aryan invaders were Macedonian Greeks*. The Macedonian Greeks are the first light-skinned race that the Indians encountered in any recorded battle. This was 326 B.C. when Alexander fought Porus and captured the territory around the east side of the Indus river and its tributaries, this was in the India of that time. This India did not include the Ganges river valley territory of today's northern India. These facts destroy the belief that the Aryans invaded India earlier than Alexander's arrival.

From this we note that Romila Thapar's supposition, expressed in her *A History of India I*, (1966) that the Aryan's invaded the Ganges area around 1500 B.C. is nonsense. This date adjustment was made by her because Mohenjo-Daro and Harappa were deemed non-Aryan cities, found in the Indus valley, that lasted from 3000 B.C. to 1500 B.C. There was no other basis for her decision to use 1500 B.C. Her adjustment changed the date from an earlier and more ridiculous pundit fabrication that the Aryan invasion was earlier than 3000 B.C.

Note: It is unlikely that the Harappans were culturally related to any Indian tribe and were certainly not Dravidians. The Harappan pinnacle is estimated at 2300 B.C. and their disintegration began about 1800 B.C. Their cities were not fortified and weapons found were primitive, which suggests they lived in peace. Each major city had a structure resembling a

> Sumerian ziggurat, built with artificial mounds of oven-baked bricks and walled at the base and a smaller circular room centered at the top. Sun-baked bricks were used in Sumeria.

Alexander the Great likely had a library built in Alexandria, Bactria (now Kandahar, Afghanistan) that led toward becoming a cultural center. The strong influence of the Bactrian Greeks on Indian culture is well documented.

Chandragupta Maurya (known as Sandracottus in Greek) proposed to Alexander a plan to continue his conquests through the Ganges valley, but Alexander had to refuse because his men wanted to return home. It is said that failing to convince his generals to continue was Alexander the Great's only defeat. Chandragupta went on to conquer the Ganges valley for himself and founded the Mauryan Dynasty. Three years after Alexander's death Chandragupta turned his power against the Greeks and finally took the Punjab into his own Empire. His grandson, Ashoka (264--227 B.C.), is regarded as one of the great political leaders in history, a compliment largely based on his so-called expressed repugnance to his war on Kalinga as well as his call to moral living expressed in the surviving Ashoka edicts engraved on columns, stones, and in caves strewn around the periphery of his Mauryan Empire. Their distribution approximates the boundaries of Ashoka's Empire. None of his edicts have been found in the central area of his Empire, which suggests that they also have a proprietary significance as boundary markers. This may also explain the choice of the various languages used in the edicts.

> **Note:** That Ashoka expressed his regret over the Kalinga revolt, where he massacred as well as exiled a large part of their population, could have been taken as a threat (there is no evidence that he returned the exiles, for example). That other communities did not want to become another one of his regrets could explain why he could reign so long without any more revolts. The decline and fall of the Mauryan Empire begins with his death.

We can deduce from Greek descriptions of Indians that Ashoka was likely as dark as the Ethiopians and therefore not Aryan. However, there was much contact with Aryans, namely with Bactrians (of Persian descent) and Greeks. These groups were regular visitors to the Mauryan court. To facilitate and encourage these visits Chandragupta built a royal road between Bactria and the Mauryan court. Furthermore, Aryans came into the northern territories by the thousands. They were regarded as welcome immigrants bringing with them their language, culture, and artisan skills.

It is said that Chandragupta wanted to purchase a Greek philosopher, but was informed that the Greeks did not sell their philosophers. The Aryans with their overbearing culture accredited by the new emperor, Chandragupta, soon eclipsed the local Indian languages and only remnants of the Dravidian languages were taken in by the Indo-European languages of the Aryans. The languages of Dravidian descent survive mostly in southern India. These facts destroy the belief that the Aryans invaded India earlier than Alexander's arrival.

The bilingual edict in the Exhibit below is neatly placed on a flattened stone in Kandahar, a city in southern Afghanistan, formerly Bactrian Greek territory. By the last line of the second language we surmise that it was written from right to left rather than left to right as the Greek is. This edict has special interest because it is written in two languages addressed toward Bactrian Greek territory, i.e., languages beyond the boundary of its placement. The second language is the *lingua franca* of ancient Persia, Aramaic, a Semitic language. This does not preclude this path for the entry of an Aryan based language. Bactria was Persian territory when Alexander arrived.

Ancient Persians used a cuneiform syllabary for their Persian inscriptions, which is likely the original 'Devanagari', but no cuneiform appears in the Ashoka edicts. A proposed but doubtful Indian candidate for 'Devanagari' script is the Kharoshthi script invented about the time of Chandragupta (c300 B.C.) and used in some of the other Western Ashoka edicts. This script derives from Aramaic and is written right to left and is likely the oldest Indian candidate. None of the edicts use the Avestan script of the Zarathustrans.

Exhibit: Ashoka edict on stone in Kandahar, Afghanistan
here showing a preference for Greek.

Most of the Ashoka edicts are unilingual but their limited variety in an Empire with so many languages suggests that at best the choice may be the administration language or regional trade language.

One edict has been translated to say that the column on which it was engraved was constructed for the purpose of this edict. The columns are smooth with a high degree of symmetry; by all appearances constructed by skilled masons (Mauryan leaders often hired Greek masons). However, the edicts on the columns look like they were engraved by amateurs. It makes one wonder whether the columns were originally intended for these edicts or just an after-thought placed on the Empire column markers of the previous leaders of the Dynasty.

Unfortunately, the reliability in the translations of the old languages leaves much in doubt and many guesses were made to get an intelligible rendering. Many of the so-called translations were based on claimed similarities to known languages. It is much like trying to translate the Iliad when all you know is modern Greek. It seems unlikely these columns made to perfection were made for the rather sloppy engravings. For scholars who demand rigor we are still hard-pressed for honest translations of the Ashoka edicts.

> **Note:** The fact that the Ashoka edicts were placed, by all appearances, arbitrarily on columns, stones, and in caves on the periphery of Ashoka's Empire suggests that they were placed on anything that was already available on that periphery.

Sanskrit, though never spoken as a natural language in India, became the adopted language of Indian intellectuals and tradition has it that its use was similar to the way Latin was used in medieval times by Europeans. Laws and Legislation were put in Sanskrit. Because they used a perishable writing material we have no sure way of following the history of these writings. We have no certain way of determining the affects of copying and recopying texts on perishable material.

When Panini constructed a Sanskrit Grammar using some 4000 Sutras it led to a devolution in the preservation of Sanskrit dialects that existed prior to his time. In effect, all dialects of Sanskrit were reduced to one artificial dialect. Indian Sanskrit pundits welcomed this unification of authority and welcomed this reduction to one dialect, as well as a number of other Panini 'simplifications'. For example, a current pundit taught me that when men speak the masculine declensions are used, when women speak the feminine declensions are used, therefore the gender of the noun form used is determined by the gender of the speaker. Panini's passion for brevity has left a number of his Sutras in a state of ambiguity and therefore obfuscation.

> **Note:** By adopting Panini's grammar the Indian pundits made Classical Sanskrit (as it came to be known) a genuine Indian construction. Through peer pressure, Panini's grammar became the statutory reference for Classical Sanskrit. Even so, except for its salient features, most Sanskrit pundits never really mastered Panini. Thus not only do we have a depravation of natural Sanskrit dialects, we have a depravation of Panini.

Few texts were left unscathed by the grammar of Panini. The Brahmins were adamant about conserving the first Sanskrit renderings of their scriptures (Rigvedas) and therefore a number of the Panini Sutras pertain only to these scriptures.

> **Note:** If these scriptures were originally in Sanskrit they were obtained by the Indian pundits from a culture other than their own. Otherwise the Brahmin sometime after the Macedonian invasion of northwestern India, on becoming literate under the Mauryan Dynasty, rendered their unwritten scriptures into Sanskrit.

Today virtually all Sanskrit texts have been affected by the Panini grammar rules and the older texts no longer recopied, being written on perishable materials, perished in time. The Panini grammar represents a kind of sterilization process that introduced a preference for passive verbs, the use of participles for verbs, and the extended use of compounding many words into one word. These compound words could substitute for sentences. That his grammar generated texts with passive verbs and multi-linked words, etc., makes it the first generative grammar. Its conciseness makes it look mathematical, resembling a transformational grammar.

> **Note:** Sir Bhandarkar compares it to geometry, "…its study possesses the educational value of the same kind as that of Euclid and not much inferior to it in degree. For to make up a particular form the mind of the student has to go through a certain process of synthesis."
>   W. D. Whitney compares it to algebra, "…Panini, whose textbook, containing the facts of the language (Sanskrit) cast into the highly artful and difficult form of about four thousand algebraic-formula-like rules…"

Studying Panini grammar resembles in important ways the study of mathematics. The Panini grammar is in effect a context free grammar that allows structures that the original natural Sanskrit would not have accepted. That it led to the destruction of many natural Sanskrit texts is documented.

Chandragupta Maurya began as an illiterate and we have no written records from his side that directly ascertain his decisions concerning language use. However, from the edicts of Ashoka, his grandson, we surmise that Greek and Persian influences had become important to the Mauryan Dynasty. We surmise that the Mauryan Empire at the time of Ashoka had within it many different languages. Today more than 300 languages are catalogued for India.

All the dominant languages of the northern Indian regions today are deemed Indo-European with an Aryan origin and are closer to ancient Persian than to Greek. Furthermore, a significant percentage of the current population in power in that area is of lighter-complexion than the black race described in Alexander's time. This suggests more than just an introduction of language literacy into the culture. We see here the beginning of Indian prejudices based on skin color associated with castes.

Again the Brahmin pundits would have us believe that the Aryans invaded the India of the Ganges, but this underestimates Chandragupta's desire to master the advantages of the Greek and Bactrian cultures, such as literacy, etc. His efforts to tolerate and assimilate these culture groups were energetic and dedicated. Witness his construction of a Royal Road between Bactria and his capitol to facilitate communications. In the early spread of Aryans across the Ganges territory, Chandragupta invited them in and even allowed them to form their own communities. This open door policy explains why there is no record of any great battles associated with these migrations. This was not an invasion, it was a migration under invitation. Many of the Bactrians coming in were Zarathustran and spoke a Persian dialect.

In the first millennium when the Zarathustran religion became an object of persecution in Bactria two large refugee groups of orthodox Zarathustrans sought refuge in India, one settled in Gujarat, maybe in the 4th Century A.D., and the other settled in Bombay, maybe in early 8th Century A.D. (Dates in a history hating culture are difficult to pinpoint). Both groups brought book collections that were part of their libraries. Refuge was granted to both groups, a continuation of a long tradition of open door policy for Aryans. These later orthodox refugee groups strictly forbid marriages of their own people to outsiders of their religion. This restriction was motivated for the survival of their religion rather than prejudice. This restriction on marriage became a problem in later generations as the spread of sterility increased through inbreeding. In effect, these later Zarathustran settlements lived in more isolation under an apartheid agreement.

The Brahmin (philosophers, priests) and Kshatriya (governors, warriors) were quick to take over the Sanskrit language and the foremost Indian Sanskrit pundits of today come from the castes formed from these groups. Concomitantly, Pakrit evolved into Pali and from the devolution of the Mauryan Dynasty the disconnection of territories prepared the way to the evolution of the languages now found in Northern India.

Critique Summary. My critique of the difficulties involved in establishing credibility to any claims upheld by verbal traditions in India does not preclude that India has produced some of the finest minds the world has known. As time goes on the list becomes longer. As with many cultures that have their civilization seated at the cross-roads of other civilizations, much of what we value in the India of today has been introduced from somewhere else. This has made India one of the world's richest countries in cultural variety and this includes over 300 different languages and dialects.

India today seems more like a shadow of the Ashokan Empire. Since Pakistan is in a border dispute with Kashmir and Kashmir is under the protection of India, no settlement is in view for Kashmir's demand for independence. Even so, there is a fairly clear dividing line between the Aryan descendants in the North and the Dravidian descendants in the South. These language groups are distinctly different. Though the New Delhi government made Hindustani the official language of India, only a minority of Indians are born to this language (Dravidians often send upper caste representatives to New Delhi that are of Aryan descent). Most Indian universities conduct courses in English, the real *lingua franca* of India. Otherwise, it would be an impasse between Aryan and Dravidian origins.

END: *Epilogue*

END: *The Pythagorean Silence*